surrounded by

spirits

© Anthony Yates Photography

About the Author

Barbara Parks is a microbiologist and podiatrist with her own private practice. She is a passionate paranormal investigator and has spoken about poltergeists in personal appearances as well as on Australian radio and television. She lives in Kalamunda, Western Australia with her husband and three children.

Books by the same author:
In the Presence of Spirits (Llewellyn 2012)
Embracing the Spirits (Llewellyn 2013)

BARBARA PARKS

surrounded by

spirits

true accounts of visits from the dead

FIRST EDITION 2015

Book design by Leila Summers
Cover art © Lario Tus – Dreamstime.com

ISBN-13: 978-1505597240
ISBN-10: 1505597242

Contact Barbara Parks:

Email: podiatrist@iinet.net.au
Facebook: www.facebook.com/BarbaraParksAuthor

PO Box 904
Kalamunda WA 6926
Australia

Printed in the United States of America

Dedication

For Neill, with love from all of us.

Acknowledgements

With much love and gratitude to all who have allowed their stories to appear in this book. Thank you for sharing what are, in many cases, intensely personal stories and for helping others glean some comfort from the telling of your post-death encounters with your loved ones.

Special thanks to my dear sister-in-law, Anthea, for allowing me to share Neill's story and to my friend, Michele, for sharing your story of losing and reconnecting with Pete. You have both endured one of life's greatest losses, yet you have emerged triumphant and strong. You have shown your family and friends that life still has its unexpected joys regardless of tragedy and loss.

Thank you to those who have openly shared their vulnerabilities, by recounting their experiences with less-than-friendly spirits. Having myself been on the receiving end of such ghostly attentions, I sympathise. Thank you for allowing me to present a balanced account of what it's like to see and interact with the spirit world.

A loving thank you to fellow author, Leila Summers, for your editing and publishing expertise. I happily chanced upon your first book whilst sick in bed, half-heartedly browsing the Kindle store. All thoughts of the flu were forgotten as I devoured your wonderful memoir within two days! Who would have thought that two years later we would be working on a book together? You are an inspiration on so many levels. Thank you!

All my love, as always, to Stuart, Eloise, Claire and Danny. Thank you for sharing this fabulous journey with me! We're truly having a ball, aren't we?

Thank you to Stirling for being unfailingly supportive and reading every word of my offerings with enthusiastic praise. Your encouragement is much appreciated!

Thank you to my readers who have connected with me at events or through social media. Your kind words and encouragement keep me inspired... and keep me tapping away when I would rather not be!

Much gratitude to the spirits (both gentle and mischievous!) who have paid me visits over the last forty-five years. I am privileged to have had contact with you, as you have completely convinced me that death is not the end. Although I didn't always appreciate your visits at the time, I wouldn't have had it any other way.

Contents

Contents

Note to the Reader

This book is a true account of my paranormal encounters. It also includes the experiences of others as told to me by family members, friends, and patients. Due to the personal nature of the stories, some names and identifying features have been changed in order to preserve the privacy of those involved.

–Barbara Parks

Introduction

Many people think of the spirit world as a far-off, mysterious dimension. They believe that spirits occupy a realm far removed from our own and that death creates an impenetrable barrier between the living and the dead.

Through the many interactions I have had with spirits, I believe otherwise. I've come to realise that the spirit world is very much a part of the physical world we live in. It's not some distant place we get shunted off to when we die, but rather a higher vibratory aspect of the world we live in now.

Although only a relatively small proportion of the population can see spirits, rest assured that spirits are everywhere. They may be silent presences who choose to go unnoticed, or they may interact with the living. The motivations for those who choose to interact are many and varied. They may wish to deliver messages of comfort, or perhaps there are unresolved issues they hope to address. Sometimes the motivation can be little more than wanting their loved ones to know that they live on.

In some instances, the spirit may feel that their death was untimely and, as such, feel reluctant to progress to the higher vibratory realms. Their death may have been sudden, premature or violent. Or perhaps they are simply too frightened to leave the world they feel most comfortable in. These souls are somehow stuck between our dense earth vibration and the higher realms of the spirit world and often manifest with a sense of sadness and negativity. This form of existence is known as the ghost state, and it is these spirits that may require help in order to wholly transition to spirit.

It seems that in days gone by, those who experienced visitations from ghosts were few and far between. Or at the very least, those who admitted to paranormal encounters were rare. Nowadays, it's apparent that more and more people are claiming to have experienced contact with the spirit world. Many believe that the veil between the spirit world and our own is now thinner than ever before, and an increasing number of people are seeking proof of this for themselves. They visit mediums, read spiritual literature or seek to develop their own psychic sensitivities. What was once a taboo has become more commonplace. It's no longer considered strange or macabre to seek contact with spirits, and belief in the spirit world has become more widely accepted.

The paranormal experiences which fill these pages, are those which I consider the most striking examples which support the reality of life after death. Some have happened to me personally, whilst others have been relayed to me by family, friends and acquaintances. The very fact that these people are willing to openly share their stories with a larger audience, vouches for their authenticity. Some have gone so far as to provide me with photographs, further enhancing the validity of their stories.

The stories within this book traverse a wide range of paranormal encounters—from the truly terrifying to the joyous and uplifting. Regardless of where they fall within this spectrum, all are reminders of the eternal nature of life and the survival of the human soul. Embracing a reality where spirits and mortals walk side by side, in my experience at least, is truly life-enhancing.

So, take a walk with me now, through the diverse corridors of the paranormal, where ordinary people like you and I have been touched by the extraordinary. Once you have been touched, you will never be the same again.

Chapter One

Neill

For my family and me, the festive season has become forever tainted. On New Year's Eve in 2013, our much loved brother-in-law, Neill, collapsed from a sudden brain haemorrhage. He was never to regain consciousness and passed away the following day.

Leaving behind his wife, Anthea, and four beautiful children made his death all the more tragic. It was difficult to comprehend that someone so young, fit and in the prime of their life could be gone so abruptly. In the lead up to his passing, there were no discernible clues that anything was amiss. A talented orthopaedic surgeon, Neill was also a keen horse-rider and surfer. He thrived in his beach-side lifestyle as much as he revelled in his successful career. But nothing surpassed the pride and love he felt for his family; he worked tirelessly to give them the very best.

Neill's passing at forty-nine years of age felt unjust and cruel; our hearts ached for both him and the family he had left behind.

My brother-in-law, Neill

Having lived two hours away from the city, Neill had been airlifted to one of the major Perth hospitals after his collapse. The family had followed by road–a fraught, angst-ridden journey that felt even worse on the way back. Returning home without Neill two days later felt painfully wrong.

Anthea worried about how she and the children would feel returning to where the tragedy had unfolded. She imagined the gaping emptiness of the family home and worried that it would be too awful to bear. The reality could not have been more different.

Whilst Anthea and the children had been in Perth, the family's troop of loyal friends had descended upon the household. Their labours had the property looking immaculate inside and out, the pantry and fridge stocked with mountains of home-made meals to see them through the difficult weeks ahead. They lined the driveway on either side as Anthea drove towards the house, forming a guard of honour as a mark of respect for both the friend they had lost and for those he had left behind.

Amongst this outpouring of love and support, more was yet to come. As Anthea entered the house itself, she was overcome by intense emotion. It wasn't the raw grief she was expecting, but rather a feeling of calm, comfort and love. She could definitely feel Neill's reassuring energy in the house, and it was an instant balm for the heartache of the last two days.

It wasn't only Anthea who felt Neill's calming energy in their home, it was as if all who passed through its doors were affected by the same feeling of healing and positivity. The house was swamped by an endless stream of visitors, and for the week we were there, I saw it happen time and time again. Grief-stricken family and friends would arrive in tears, only to be happily smiling mere moments later. All agreed that there was a beautiful, warm feeling in the home. And at least for me, I had no doubt where it was coming from.

My suspicions were confirmed on the day we arrived, which was two days after Neill's passing. At first I saw a pale, luminescent figure lingering in the kitchen doorway. He seemed to be flanking Mark, who was one of Neill's dearest friends.

I told Mark what I was seeing and suggested we should grab a camera to see if Neill wanted to show himself in our photos. Neill obliged, showing himself as a small, bright orb just behind Mark's left shoulder.

I praised Neill, but suggested he could do better. I asked him to accompany me to the family room and coached him as to how to show himself more vividly in photographs. I told him I would count out loud and that he should try to coincide flashing his spirit light on the count of three. I poised my camera and began to count.

I immediately knew that I had captured something special. As well as capturing the most vivid, radiant orb I had ever seen, there were dozens of smaller orbs in the photo as well. It seemed that Neill was surrounded by a small army of spirit guides—his own personal entourage who were guiding him on his journey. Seeing this beautiful display of spirit energy filled me with extreme joy!

Two days after his passing, Neill was able to garner his spirit energy in order to show himself to us as a radiant spirit orb. His surrounding entourage of spirit guides makes this photograph all the more comforting.

I told Neill that I was impressed, but now I hoped to take it to another level. I needed to prove to myself (and to the others) that I was really communicating with him. The best way to do this was to try to develop some sort of interaction beyond just one photograph.

"Neill…I think you should know that your brothers-in-law and best mates are planning on cracking open that expensive old whiskey of yours. You know the one you've been saving for years? Well, they're planning on drinking it tonight!"

I focussed the camera on Neill's bar area, where the expensive bottle lay in wait.

"So what do you think about that?" I asked.

When talk turned to partaking in Neill's prized bottle of whiskey, he was quick to whiz down from his vantage point near the ceiling to position himself on the bottle.

I counted to three and SNAP! There he was. The same beautiful orb which had graced my previous photograph had left its place near the ceiling and had repositioned itself on the prized bottle. All I could do was laugh. I jokingly asked Neill if he was guarding the bottle from being consumed by his buddies or if he was giving them the seal of approval. I felt sure that it was the latter.

"Are you joining them for a drink then?" I asked. The beautiful flash of light in response made it clear that he approved.

"Well, in that case, I'd better join you too!"

It was a lovely drop indeed, made all the sweeter by the fact that we knew Neill was sharing the moment with us.

The weeks that followed were by no means easy, especially for Anthea and the children. Yet despite the grief that needed to be endured, there was an underlying sense of comfort in knowing that Neill was still around. We still shed our tears and struggled to comprehend that such a terrible thing had happened, but we knew that he hadn't really left us. I looked at Neill's orb photos often in those sad, early days and appreciated having a tangible reminder that life goes on regardless. It goes on for those who have died and for those left behind—beautiful in its own way on both sides of the veil.

Another Visit

A few months went by without incident, as I imagine Neill focussed on his new life in the spirit world and we forged on without him. When he eventually made contact, it was sudden, unexpected and very welcome.

I had been asked to help a recently bereaved widow make contact with her husband and arranged to conduct a séance in her home. The husband's name was Dan, and he had been a general practitioner.

The séance was proceeding beautifully, with Dan providing one validation after another, convincing his wife that his spirit lived on. Then, quite out of nowhere, Dan began speaking about someone named Neill. I caught my breath.

Dan's wife said she had no idea whom he was talking about, as she couldn't recall Dan knowing anyone called Neill. She thought it bizarre that after all the valid information he had provided, Dan was now throwing a name in the ring that didn't seem to make sense.

"I know a Neill," I told her. "I'm really sorry, but I think your reading is about to be hijacked. Do you mind if I ask Dan a couple of questions?"

"Go for it!" she smiled.

I asked Dan if he'd known Neill whilst they were alive and he said that he hadn't. He told me that he'd only just met him and that he was connected to me. My heart began to beat faster.

"Do you know what Neill did as a profession?" I asked.

YES... ORTHOPAEDIC SURGEON.

I couldn't help smiling as I apologised to my sitter. I told her that Neill was my brother-in-law and asked if I could have a quick word with him before we got back to her husband. She had no problem with that at all and was happy for Neill to step in and say his piece.

We only spoke briefly as Neill was mindful of gate-crashing someone else's reading. He was very keen for me to arrange a reading with Anthea and the children and asked me to do so soon. He assured me that he was okay and was pleased that his family seemed to be getting on with life without him.

I promised I would call Anthea as soon as I got home and that he would have the opportunity to speak to his family again soon. At that, we bid each other farewell and I returned my attention to Dan.

I couldn't wait to get home and give my sister-in-law a call.

"Ants!" I said as she answered her mobile. "Are you sitting down?"

"No... I'm driving. Why?"

"Just pull over. Something amazing just happened!"

A moment later I was telling Anthea the full story, leaving her as gobsmacked as I had been when Neill first stepped in. We made arrangements for me to come and do the reading in two weeks' time. Since Anthea and the children lived over two hundred kilometres away, it was decided that I would stay for the weekend.

So on a rainy Saturday afternoon, we gathered in the sitting room just outside Neill and Anthea's bedroom. We lit a white candle, closed our eyes and began to breathe deeply, silently meditating as we waited for Neill to come forward.

With very little coaxing, the messages began to filter through—personal, heartfelt assurances that everything was okay. He told the family he missed them and freely expressed his love. They took turns asking him questions, and he was quick to respond. After a few minutes, Neill focussed his attentions on seventeen-year-old Charlotte.

CHARLOTTE... NO NO NO...

"What do you mean, Dad?" she asked.

Neill kept repeating *NO,* after which he told her to *GET A RING.*

We had no idea what he was trying to tell us, and Anthea asked him if he could be more specific.

CHARLOTTE FINGER... NO NO NO! He replied. *GET A RING!*

I looked at Anthea and shrugged.

"It's just not making any sense at all..."

Charlotte began to look uneasy, and she told us that the message actually made perfect sense. She confessed to having plans to get a tattoo–a tattoo which commemorated her father by having his birth and death dates encircling her finger.

"So you want me to have them engraved on a ring instead?" she asked tearfully.

YES! Neill answered.

We were all amused by the fact that Neill was dobbing on his daughter from beyond the grave. Had Charlotte gone ahead with her tattoo plan, Anthea would have been mortified. A pretty ring to commemorate her father was a much better idea!

We wound up proceedings on a high note, having teased Neill about being a dobber and still having control over his kids. The fact that Neill knew about Charlotte's secret plan was a wonderful validation that he was still involved in his family's lives. I wonder if his impatience to instigate a reading was for the purpose of curtailing Charlotte's tattoo plan. Or was he just eager to reassure them that he had never really left? Whatever the motive, Neill's visit left a feeling of calm and happiness in its wake. As we popped the cork of a bottle of expensive French champagne, we felt certain that Neill was close by. Had we had a camera handy, we may well have seen his beautiful spirit light shining on the bottle!

As we sipped in silence, we smiled in gratitude for what we had just experienced. We were celebrating Neill's life, his transition to spirit and the fact that he was still a part of our lives.

Chapter Two

From the Mouths of Babes

Some signs from spirits are so astonishing that they seem far-fetched in the retelling. This is one such story—and as incredible as it may sound—you can rest assured, it is true.

Yvonne approached me at the end of one of my spirit contact seminars, as she wanted to share a story of her own. We had just spent the evening in the cellar of an old hotel and the mood was primed for all things paranormal. The cellar was abuzz with the energy of spirits; it was the perfect setting for sharing stories from beyond.

Yvonne told me that it wasn't so long ago that her friend's young daughter passed away after a protracted battle with cancer. Nine-year-old Jessica had been becoming progressively weaker and her prognosis bleaker, yet the more her physical state deteriorated, the more peaceful she seemed to be. Although Jess had been terrified at the prospect of dying, she seemed to have suddenly done a complete turnaround. It was baffling to her parents, but they were grateful for whatever was responsible for their daughter's newfound calm.

As the days went by, it seemed that Jess became aware of unseen presences in the room. Her mother watched quietly from the sidelines, as Jess smiled and interacted with her invisible friends. It all came to a head one evening as Jess's frail little form lay wallowing in the bathtub. She became so animated and giggly that her mother just had to know what was going on. She asked her daughter whom she was talking to.

"It's the beautiful ladies," smiled Jess. "They're looking after me!"

Jess went on to tell her mother that there were three white ladies in the bathroom. As she described them, they sounded very much like angels. They had assured Jess that they would never leave her and that, when the time came, they would guide her on her journey. They promised that Jess had nothing to be afraid of.

Her mother was stunned. Although hopeful, she was unsure as to whether the angels were real. It was hard not to presume that they were figments of the child's imagination—a possible protective mechanism to ease her through an inconceivable trauma. But as time went on, she became more and more convinced. Observing Jess's interactions with the invisible ladies left her in little doubt. Jess was animated and happy. It was a glimpse back to how Jess had been before she became ill. Most tellingly, her mother couldn't deny that the interactions were accompanied by a feeling of love and peacefulness in the room. It was as though the angels were bringing comfort, not only to Jess, but to everyone in the household.

In the lead up to Jess's death, it was a great comfort to know that Jess wouldn't be embarking on the next phase of her journey alone. Her mother had every faith that her darling daughter would be lovingly guided by the three beautiful angels. Of course Jess herself had no fear whatsoever.

Her health continued to deteriorate, and she passed away within weeks. In the lead up to her death, she continued to talk about the unwavering presence of the angels.

Although the pain of her passing was devastating, the family reminded themselves that Jess was now happy and pain-free. They planned a joyous celebration of her life, culminating with the release of a mass of purple helium balloons. Purple was her favourite colour. The balloons dotted the azure blue sky, until they were little more than tiny specks on the horizon. The congregation stood watching as they gradually disappeared from sight.

The flurry of activity that normally follows someone's passing gradually receded, as family and friends tried to fall back into some semblance of normality. Although the family's support network was still very much intact, it was during this post-funeral lull that Jess's mother began to truly absorb the gravity of her loss. With all the formalities over, it seemed that she was now expected to get on with her life without Jess. It seemed impossible.

Whilst driving in her car and feeling particularly fragile, Jess's mother realised that she wasn't far from the church where Jess's funeral had been. The realisation struck her like a slap to the face, as a myriad of painful memories began to flood in. As strong as she had been, there were times she would crumble with a single memory and now they were coming in thick and fast. She pulled over to the side of the road to try and compose herself.

Fighting back the tears, she asked her daughter for a sign—anything that would prove to her that she was still around.

Jess must've been ready and waiting, as this is where the story transcends the commonplace. What happened next was nothing short of magical! Seemingly appearing out of nowhere, a purple helium balloon floated into sight. As if that wasn't enough, it wafted over on a gentle breeze and sailed right into the car through her mother's open window.

Her mother's grief-stricken tears were replaced by tears of joy; the balloon was most certainly a gift from Jessica!

She drove home with the bobbing balloon by her side, smiling from ear to ear. She couldn't wait to tell her family.

As Jess's story attests, the spirit world is more incredible than we can ever truly fathom. Spirits will go to great lengths to engineer events which will comfort their loved ones; proving that they are still with us is high on their list of priorities. The signs may not always be as dramatic as Jess's purple balloon, but they are just as precious nonetheless. We need to be open and receptive and keep our senses primed so as not to miss the signs that our loved ones are close by.

As far as Jess goes, I wonder if she had any help in orchestrating such an amazing display for her mother. Perhaps it was all her own doing, or maybe she had a little help. After all, she does have friends in high places... at least three such friends that I know of!

Chapter Three

Preshti

I've long believed that synchronicities are signs from the spirit world. Sometimes events play out in such a meant-to-be, seamless fashion, that it seems they are being engineered from the other side. That's how it felt when I met Preshti.

It was a cool spring morning as I strolled the main street of Kalamunda, pondering the plight of some earthbound spirits I'd recently encountered. Although I knew they wanted to cross over, I was unsure as to how to go about helping such a large group of ghosts. Feeling overwhelmed by the task before me, I decided to call on my friend, Sherrie, who worked in the local florist shop. Perhaps sharing a coffee and a chat would offer me some clarity. I needed some direction and hoped that talking about the situation would help me to feel more centred.

I entered the shop to find Sherrie busily working on an arrangement with a petite Indian lady watching from close by. The woman looked almost ethereal with her wavy, waist-length hair and beautiful, radiant face. She smiled as I edged in beside her, negotiating my way around Sherrie's gorgeous tubs of blooms.

"Wow!" I said, admiring Sherrie's handiwork. "How absolutely gorgeous!"

"They're for Preshti," she smiled with a nod towards the woman.

Preshti turned to me and offered her hand, all the while smiling broadly as we introduced ourselves. She told me that she was a nutritionist and was catering a special event later that day. The flowers were an added personal touch that she hoped would please her clients.

Our conversation was initially centred on nutrition, and Preshti told me how passionate she was about wholefoods which nurture both the body and the spirit. She told me that she had been diagnosed with uterine cancer some years ago and had opted to treat herself purely through diet, exercise and meditation. She refused any form of medical intervention, preferring to refine her diet and lifestyle, which she did with amazing results. Her doctors were astounded when follow-up scans showed no signs of the once-invasive cancer.

She had since made a great success of her career as a nutritionist. Preshti asked about my own profession, and I told her that I had recently sold my podiatry practice in preference for focussing on my career as a writer. When I told her about the subject matter of my books, her face lit up.

"So you see spirits?" she asked.

I nodded.

"Me too..." she said.

And as though someone had suddenly opened the floodgates to her secrets, Preshti began telling me story after story about her ghostly companions, the first of which made himself known to her when she was a very young girl.

"He'd be everywhere," she told me. "This big, tall guy with a beard and he looked as solid as we do. He'd either stand in my doorway, or in the corner of my room. If I told him to go away, he'd just stand outside my bedroom and stare at me through my window."

"Ugh!" I said. "That sounds creepy..."

"Well, yeah, it was really scary at the time because I had no idea who he was. As it turns out he's actually my spirit guide, he just hadn't announced himself yet!"

Preshti told me that she now has a very close relationship with her guide and that he manifests as a solid, physical being. He speaks to her so clearly that his voice is as tangible as that of a living person.

"And my brother visits me too," she smiled. "He passed away a few years ago. He'll sit on the end of my bed and talk to me for hours, it's like he never even left!"

The more she spoke, the more I understood how Preshti's history had helped mould the highly spiritual person she is today. Although clairvoyant since birth, it seems her life's traumas had heightened her sensitivity. Facing a terminal illness and the death of her brother had somehow enriched and shaped the beautiful person she had become. It's heartening to see something so wonderful emerge as the result of painful, dark times.

It's long been believed that trauma can heighten paranormal abilities. If you were to probe the personal histories of the world's most gifted mediums and clairvoyants, you would often see a discernible pattern of adversity unfold. Preshti was no exception.

I told Preshti a little about my own experiences, which I believed were borne of the fact that I almost died at birth. We discussed my still-limited clairvoyance, and I expressed my dismay at not being able to hear my ghostly visitors. She assured me that with time, it would come.

She did, however, warn me to be careful what I wished for. It seems that once the doors of communication with the spirit world are opened, a steady stream of ghostly visitors is likely to beat a path to your door.

"They track me down everywhere!" she laughed.

Preshti described an encounter whereby she returned to her car after an outing, to find an elderly native woman waiting in the passenger seat.

"At first I thought she was real and that she might have been about to steal my car," said Preshti. "Anyway, once I realised she was a ghost, I got in beside her and asked her what she wanted. It seemed she didn't quite grasp that she was dead."

The old woman proceeded to talk to Preshti for two hours, lamenting the treatment of herself and her people in the historic, nearby prison. She wanted it to be known that they had not been treated fairly—a situation that may have explained her reluctance to move on.

After much soothing and reassurance, Preshti managed to convince the woman that now that her life's injustices had been openly acknowledged, it was time to put them behind her and move on. Lingering at the scene of her mistreatment would only fuel her unhappiness.

"It took a while, but she eventually agreed to transition. I asked her whom she wanted me to send for, and she told me the names of some relatives she thought might be waiting for her. Sure enough, they all came to help her cross over!"

"So you're actually able to cross over spirits?" I asked.

I must've been staring at Preshti with ill-disguised awe, as she suddenly began to laugh.

"Most of the time I can," she replied. "Let's just say that some spirits cross over more readily than others."

Preshti went on to tell me about a deceased husband and wife who occupied her bedroom for a week before they finally crossed over. Being a teenager at the time, she found the experience extremely disturbing, especially since her visitors harboured the wounds which lead to their untimely deaths.

"They'd been in a car accident," said Preshti with a shudder. "The man had half of his face missing, and his wife didn't look much better."

Since they were displaying the injuries sustained by their physical bodies, Preshti knew that the couple were earthbound ghosts. Once the dead cross over into the higher realms of the spirit world, they revert to appearing healthy and unblemished, whereas these poor souls looked terrifyingly disfigured.

"They kept asking me for help," said Preshti. "It was as if they thought I could make them better. It was awful!"

"I asked them where the accident had happened, as I imagined that it must have been close by. They were confused and said that they didn't know where or when the accident had taken place. All they knew was that they had been told to come to me and that I'd be able to help them."

When Preshti asked the ghosts who exactly had sent them, they simply replied, "They did." To this day, she still doesn't know where her frequent ghostly referrals keep coming from.

"The word must be filtering through the ether," I said. "You probably have quite a reputation!"

"Maybe," said Preshti, looking thoughtful. I could see that she was still affected by the memory of the ghosts.

"So did they cross over?" I asked.

"Eventually," she said. "But it took more than a little persuasion."

It transpired that the couple had three young children, and they couldn't bear to leave them. They believed that if they crossed over, they would be trapped in the higher dimensions forever. They thought that they would no longer be able to see their children if they went into the light.

In reality, they were more trapped by remaining in the astral plane than they would be when they crossed over. Once a soul progresses to the higher realms, it is more able to travel between dimensions. So even though they would be existing in a higher vibrational, enlightened state, there was nothing to prevent them from assuming a role of protection and guidance in their three children's lives. In fact, many people have spirit guides who are deceased relatives who have undertaken this role after their physical deaths.

"So anyway, after about a week I finally managed to help them," said Preshti. "The thing is, as much as I want to help souls cross over, I can't just force them. They have to want to go."

"And then what?" I asked. "Do you just conjure the light for them?"

"Well, there are a couple of ways you can do it. I always ask if there's anyone in spirit that they would like to come and get them. They'll usually ask for a grandparent or parent, or some other family member or friend. If they're confused and unsure who to call on, you can just summon Archangel Michael. The angels always come when you need them. He'll ward off any negativity and draw them into the light. Another thing you can do is visualize a big, beautiful column of intense light reaching upwards... that seems to work too!"

So here we were, still in the middle of a florist shop, having the deepest conversation imaginable. Sherrie had long since finished with her flower arrangement and was as absorbed in Preshti's story as I was.

"I think you might need a mentor," said Preshti with a smile. "Is this what you want to do? Are you ready to start working with spirit?"

"I've been ready for ages," I said.

"Well then, perhaps we met here today for a reason."

She took my business card and slipped it into her handbag. Sherrie handed her the beautiful bunch of flowers, which all but dwarfed her diminutive frame.

"I think I might just have to call you," she said as she breezed her way out of the shop. "If you need me, I'll know!"

Then, as swiftly and unexpectedly as she had appeared in my life half an hour earlier, she disappeared through the door with a flourish. Sherrie and I looked at each other and smiled.

"Whoa!" I laughed. "What do you make of that?"

"Amazing!" said Sherrie.

It was a case of synchronicity at its best. I had come by hoping to debrief with a dear friend over a cup of coffee, but had come away with so much more than I'd expected. I felt as though the powers that be knew exactly what I needed and decided to help me along. It was humbling and awe-inspiring.

I suddenly felt as though anything was possible, even helping the earthbound ghosts. I hoped that now that I had sown the seeds towards fulfilling this goal, I was a little closer to helping the lost souls I came into contact with. If it proved beyond my capabilities, I had just met someone who could undoubtedly help. The prospect of crossing over souls now felt within my reach, and I was poised and ready to help!

Chapter Four

A Wonderful Séance

Given that I'm well-versed in the inherent risks of séances, many people find it surprising that I conduct them so regularly. There are times when I question whether I'm doing the right thing, to the point where I take a break from them for a while. Then invariably someone comes along with a heartfelt request to contact someone in spirit, and before I know it, I find myself reaching out to the spirit world once again. In some instances, it is the spirits themselves who seek me out. I find these requests particularly hard to refuse, as I know how much comfort and happiness can come from facilitating such communications.

My most recent séance gave rise to one such interaction, whereby the room was filled with a sense of joy as the messages began to flood in. It reinforced my belief that when conducted lovingly, responsibly and safely, the séance can indeed be a wonderful gift.

I met Michele briefly in my early twenties, after which our paths didn't cross again for two decades. In the intervening years, Michele married her sweetheart, Pete, and they had three gorgeous children.

Nine years into their marriage, they were struck by a cruel and unexpected blow. Without any warning whatsoever, Pete passed away shortly after retiring to bed one night. For reasons that will never be fully understood, Pete began to fit and had difficulty breathing. Despite Michele's immediate first aid, nothing could be done to save him. He was forty-four years old.

Pete's sudden passing at forty-four years of age left his wife, Michele, and their three children devastated.

I crossed paths with Michele four years after Pete's death, by which time she had met her new partner, Sean. Although still carrying the deep scars of her loss, she was conducting her life exactly as Pete would have wanted. She was a devoted, nurturing mother and a successful businesswoman. She was purposefully moving forward with her life, whilst keeping Pete's memory alive for both herself and her children.

The family spoke of Pete often and suspected that he called in from time to time to check up on things. There were numerous signs that Pete was around, never more so than when there was a camera close by.

Michele (seated cross-legged on the lounge) is convinced that the large orb beside her is Pete.

As well as frequently appearing as a brilliant orb in family photographs, Pete also saw fit to put in appearances in video recordings. One home movie is particularly amusing. It contains footage of the family piling on top of each other as they play the raucous game of Stacks On. The video shows the children squealing delightedly as they clamber on top of one another (all the while being tickled by a giggling Michele), as a baseball-sized orb darts around them. The orb skims over and around the family, with an exuberance fuelled by the joy in the room.

It wasn't unusual for photos of Michele and the children to have an orb hovering close by. The family feel sure that Pete is still very much a part of their lives.

Michele also recounts small, inexplicable events which the family have come to accept as signs from Pete. Balls have spontaneously rolled across the floor, and from time to time certain members of the family (including Sean) have been lucky enough to see a fleeting figure. It was comforting to know that Pete was around.

When I approached Michele with the offer of trying to communicate with Pete, she accepted without hesitation. She had every faith that Pete would jump at the chance to make contact.

Michele turned up with a beautiful arrangement of orchids and her ever-present smile. We both knew it was going to be a memorable afternoon. We sat chatting before starting the séance and I warned Michele that there was no guarantee that whomever she was expecting was going to join us at the table. There was no pretence as to whom we were hoping to speak to, and I hoped with all my heart that Pete would turn up.

I also warned her with regard to the possibility of a mischievous ghost possibly impersonating Pete. Sometimes a wayward entity can chance across a séance and decide to get up to a little mischief. These ghosts may pretend to be someone else, both for the purposes of their amusement and as a way to get attention. Although a rare occurrence, it's nonetheless something to be mindful of. In order to ascertain whether the spirit is really whom they claim to be,

I advise my sitters to ask a definitive question that only their deceased loved one would know the answer to. I recommend that the question be something very personal, the answer of which is preferably only known to the spirit and the sitter.

Such questions also serve another important purpose—they validate my authenticity as a medium. There have been occasions whereby I've been accused of obtaining my information off the internet, rather than channelling true messages from spirit. When doubt is cast on the authenticity of the communication, it is not only upsetting for me, but also for the spirit. My ego recovers, but I feel sorry for the spirits who have had their messages doubted or dismissed. So for everyone's sake, I suggest that my sitters think of a *secret question*—something which will eliminate all doubt as to the genuineness of the communication.

Thus briefed, Michele and I took our places at the table. As is my usual practice, I took some time focussing my energy as I filled the room with white light. I always take this precaution to reduce the possibility of negative energy getting through. I also invite my guides (and those of my sitter) to draw in beside us and act as gatekeepers, thereby filtering who is permitted to make contact.

It wasn't long before I felt the subtle vibration of energy coursing through my fingertips—my sure sign that a spirit was ready to make contact. Michele and I placed our fingers on the planchette and invited the spirit to identify himself.

After a slow start, the planchette began to effortlessly move around the table. He told us it was Pete.

"Middle name?" I asked.

MICHAEL.

By Michele's tears, I knew this was correct. The couple proceeded to engage in a tearful (though joyous) conversation, and Pete assured his wife that he was still a part of her life. He told her that as abrupt and shocking as his death had been, it was part of his pre-ordained life's journey. On a soul level, he'd known it was coming all along. And whilst he was busily occupied and thriving in the spirit world, he still checked in on his family to ensure they were okay. He told her that he loved her time and time again.

I reminded Michele to ask Pete her secret question.

"Ah yes!" she smiled. "Pete, tell me the name of the dog you hated... the dog that used to dig up the backyard."

WILSON, he answered without a moment's hesitation.

"And what breed was he?"

RED KELPIE.

On both counts, he was absolutely correct. Michele and I smiled at each other across the table.

As the séance progressed, the mood in the room became increasingly joyous. The couple were delighted to be speaking to each other once again. I did, however, notice that the energy was starting to dwindle. It seemed that Pete was beginning to get tired. Before drawing the communication to a close, I asked Pete if there was anything further he wanted to say.

YES... QUESTION.

"You have a question for Michele?" I asked.

YES.

"Okay... go for it."

WILL YOU MARRY?

"Do you want me to?" asked Michele tearfully.

The planchette wasted no time moving to the *YES*.

"Do you know Michele's new partner's name?" I asked.

YES... SEAN.

"So you want Michele to marry Sean?"

YES!

Although it was a heart-rending exchange, there was no mistaking Pete's support of Michele remarrying. Michele later told me that she and Sean had indeed been discussing marriage, and it was lovely to know that Pete was supportive of their plans. Pete also told us that the family would be moving house and named the very suburb in which the couple had been searching for a new home.

As Pete stepped back, we assured him we would chat again sometime in the future. In the meantime, it was heartening to know that his loving presence was still enmeshed within the family home.

Happier Days: Sean and Michele were delighted to have Pete's blessing.

Before drawing the séance to a close, I asked if there was anyone else present who wanted to speak to Michele.

YES.

"And you are?"

EMMETT.

Michele burst into tears once again. Emmett had been a good friend of both Michele and Pete's and had died just over a year ago from a sudden brain aneurysm.

Emmett was full of love and Irish good humour and told us that he and Pete had been playing cards. He also mentioned his nephew, Niall, and said that he sometimes joined the lads for poker too.

We found this odd, as Niall is still very much alive. The thirty-something Niall had been incredibly close to his uncle and was devastated by his untimely passing. I asked if Niall had been hanging out with Emmett on the astral plane as I thought that perhaps he was astral travelling in his sleep. Emmett confirmed this to be true. Sleep-state interactions with deceased loved ones are often dismissed as dreams, but in many instances the living and the dead do indeed fraternize during sleep. The experiencer often awakens with the feeling that they have just had the best dream about their loved one, little realising that they have in fact been blessed with a true spirit visitation. I suggested that Michele asks Niall whether he's had any poker-playing dreams about his beloved uncle.

Through the course of the communication, I noticed a figure standing just off to my left. Every so often, a vivid purple light would flash from where he was standing.

"Is that you, Emmett?" I asked. "Are you flashing a beautiful purple light at me?"

YES.

"And what does the purple signify?"

FAITH.

Michele smiled and told me that despite being raised as a Catholic, Emmett had never really embraced his religion or the concept of life after death. Whilst alive, Emmett believed that when you died, that was it; there was nothing beyond the physical existence. It seemed that by showing the colour purple, Emmett was trying to say that faith is indeed a virtue. It portends a belief in the afterlife, which he has since discovered to be very real.

Emmett's demeanour was very charming, and I asked him if he had the looks to match. He readily confirmed that he certainly did.

"So what would you rate yourself out of ten?" I asked jokingly.

8

"Hahaha... cool! And what would you rate Pete then?"

7

Michele and I began to laugh. Before we drew the séance to a close, it was time to ask the secret question.

"Okay," said Michele. "What was that nickname you used to call me? Especially when you'd send me a text message..."

The planchette whizzed across the table with obvious glee.

FOXY LADY.

"That's right!" laughed Michele.

I asked Emmett if he had anything further to say before signing off, and the planchette skimmed across to YES almost before I'd finished the question.

BRING CATH, he said.

Michele told me that Cath is Emmett's wife.

"But what if I were to tell you that I'm retiring and won't be doing these sessions anymore?" I asked him teasingly. "What would you say to that?"

NO!

"Fine then," I laughed.

"I suppose you'd better bring Cath," I said to Michele.

As the session came to a close, Michele and I truly felt as though we'd just spent the afternoon with two charming gentlemen. They were funny, engaging and loving, and most heartening of all, they were happy.

So when it seems as though conducting séances is too risky, too time-consuming, too draining or too whatever, séances such as my session with Michele make my resolve to quit difficult to adhere to. Speaking with deceased loved ones not only brings great comfort and healing, it demystifies the great divide between the living and the dead. Death is little more than a physical event–an event which has no hope of severing the bonds of love which bind us to our loved ones.

Whilst it's often said that life is beautiful, so too is death. Spirits like Pete and Emmett have convinced me of that. So whilst death is indeed perceived as the great unknown (and approaching the unknown can feel frightening), something tells me that when the time comes, death doesn't feel so 'unknown' after all. It's a return to the dimension we originally came from, and homecomings are nothing short of joyous.

Addendum: Two weeks after this séance, I honoured Emmett's wish by inviting Cath to come for a sitting. True to his promise, Emmett seized the opportunity to speak to his wife, assuring her that he was fine. He provided names and personal details that only he could have known, thereby convincing his wife that his spirit lived on. Although he told us that he frequently visited the family home, he made it known that he was also busy 'elsewhere'. The over-riding message was that he remained a part of his family's lives, whilst simultaneously continuing on his own spiritual journey.

Chapter Five

Signs from the Spirits

Departed loved ones will often go to great lengths to assure their families that they are still around them. The signs of their continued existence can, however, be very subtle, so much so that we miss them altogether. Others are much more obvious–their calling cards from the spirit world often hitting us like a ton of bricks. They are the signs which leave us in no doubt that our spirit family are around us and have the propensity to be life-changing. At the very least, they are a soothing balm to our grief, as we cannot help but believe that our loved ones are near.

My parents had one such experience and were privileged to receive a sign so convincing that it had them (along with everyone else present at their dinner table) in tears.

Mum and Dad emigrated from Croatia in 1967, leaving behind their parents and siblings in search of a new beginning in Australia. My paternal grandfather, Duro, had already passed some years earlier, whereas my remaining grandparents passed away during my parents' absence. It is one of the greatest pains of living abroad–not knowing if you will ever see your family again. As it turned out, it was ten years before they returned to Croatia for the first time. By then, my maternal grandfather was also dead.

In recent times, my parents have endeavoured to return to their homeland as often as finances allow–their latest trip home being a few months ago. Although all my grandparents have long since died, my father's two sisters and brother still live in Croatia. Spending time with them is their greatest motive for returning. It's always a wonderful celebration when the four siblings reunite, although there is an undeniable sense of sorrow that their parents are no longer alive.

In celebration of the recent rare event of the four siblings being together, they arranged to go on a family trip to Hungary. It was to be just the four Margaretic 'children' and their spouses. As it was the first time the four siblings had been together in years, it was a much anticipated and joyous occasion.

They made a booking at one of Hungary's most highly acclaimed and oldest restaurants, *Matyas Pince*, and settled in for an evening of fine food and music. A group of gypsy musicians wandered from table to table, regaling the diners with heartfelt Hungarian music. Armed with their violins, their music filled the dining room with a mixture of joy, heartache and passion.

As they made their way to my family's table, the musicians burst into a familiar heart-rending melody—it was my Grandfather Duro's favourite song. My father and his siblings were overwhelmed; they couldn't believe the startling synchronicity that had just occurred. It was a song they hadn't heard for years, and now they were being serenaded by its melancholic splendour.

They all privately hoped that the song was a sign that their adored father was with them in spirit, but of course logic told them that it was just a happy coincidence. Until, that is, the next song began to play.

It was a song from a Croatian operetta called *Grofica Marica*, and it had been their mother's favourite song.

"By now, we were all crying," said my mother. "Siblings and spouses alike... we recognised it straight away!"

Even recalling the story now, my father gets emotional. The coincidence was just too obscure, particularly since they were in a foreign country at the time and those were the only two Croatian songs played through the course of the entire evening. The gypsy musicians hadn't even been aware that my father's family were Croatian—the chances of it happening were miniscule.

What was always going to be a special night had become even more so. My father and his siblings were convinced that their parents were around, delighting in a rare reunion of their four beloved children!

How spirits actually engineer such events is hard for our mortal minds to understand. Spirits are essentially energy, so manipulating other forms of energy is probably quite straightforward for them. Manipulating lights (by either turning them on or off, or causing them to flicker) is one of the most common signs from spirit, as are radios, computers and televisions being tampered with. Understanding how spirits can influence music is harder to comprehend. Perhaps they can subtly influence the minds of the musicians, similar to how a spirit can convey a psychic message. We can only hypothesize about the ways in which spirits affect the material world, until we inhabit the spirit world ourselves. For now, all we can do is acknowledge the signs and enjoy them!

Perhaps less bizarre, but equally remarkable, were the signs I received from my dear friend, Deni, after his passing. In the early months after his death, I was entirely consumed by my grief. Deni did his best to let me know that he was there, by turning on the radio to full blast and tugging on my clothing. It was all done in such a way to convey his playfulness and good humour. The signs he offered assured me that, other than being dead, he hadn't really changed at all. It was just the comfort I needed in the midst of my intense grief.

It is often in this intense, post-death period when grief is at its peak, that our loved ones are most eager to comfort us. However, it takes something pretty vivid to get our attention, as we are quite often numbed by our loss. Our senses may not be as primed as they would be without the fogginess of our grief, so our spirit friends may need to do something rather striking to capture our attention. Fortunately for some, they quite often do.

A lady named Carol contacted me via my web page to tell me about some experiences her family had, following the death of her grandfather, Ron. The most memorable encounter centred on a pair of treasured earrings—earrings which became even more precious following the day of her grandfather's death.

Carol's mother was on a mercy dash to Adelaide with her brother and his wife. Their father was on his deathbed several hundred miles away, and they were hoping to reach him before he died. The three travellers bundled into their car and set off on their sad journey.

On their final stop before Adelaide, they stopped at a roadhouse to shower and freshen up. Not long after setting off for the final leg of their journey, Carol's mother was dismayed to discover she had lost her precious earrings. She frantically scoured the car, but there was no sign of them.

With a sick feeling in her stomach, Carol's mother came to the only possible conclusion—she had left the earrings behind at the roadhouse. There was no time to turn back.

By the time the threesome reached Adelaide a few hours later, they discovered that Ron had already died. His time of death coincided exactly with the time they had made their fateful pit stop. Not only had Carol's mother lost her precious father, but she had also lost her favourite earrings at the exact same moment.

Feeling gutted, they sat by the old gent's bedside and said their farewells—a little late perhaps—but at least they were able to pay their final respects. They returned to the car with wet eyes and heavy hearts.

And then, in a split second, intense grief gave way to disbelief and awe. Carol's mother was the first to see them and could hardly believe her eyes. There on the car seat lay her precious pair of earrings, carefully placed side-by-side. It could only have been a sign from her father.

"There was just no other explanation," said Carol. "They'd searched the car from top to bottom before reaching the hospital, and the earrings definitely weren't there!"

Carol's family were convinced that the return of her mother's earrings had been a gift from Ron. It was his way of showing his love as he said his final goodbye.

Even now, several years later, the family still talk about the mysterious return of the earrings. Whenever something goes right against all odds, the family are always quick to thank their old dad and granddad. They are sure he is still keeping an eye on them from the other side.

The reappearance of the lost earrings, or indeed any objects which spontaneously materialise from another location, are referred to as 'apports'. The mode by which this process occurs is unable to be explained through science, but has been reported enough throughout history for the phenomenon to be recognised as being real. It is believed that spirit energy (and in particular the energy associated with poltergeists) is able to deconstruct the molecular structure of an object in one location and reconstruct it in another, thereby giving the illusion that an object has simply appeared out of nowhere. Carol's family's earring case was likely to have been a classic case of an apport.

As far as poltergeist activity goes, for some reason it appears that these ghosts have a particular fondness for hiding car keys. Perhaps it's because they know that their disappearance will more than likely incite a reaction. The keys can disappear from their usual hook or hallway table, reappearing in obscure places such as the top of a cupboard or behind the toilet. These types of apports are all about getting a reaction.

More benevolent examples of spontaneously appearing/disappearing objects are often associated with departed loved ones. The most common of these involve feathers and coins.

A dear friend of mine had such an experience whilst sitting in an empty cathedral praying. She had recently commenced chemotherapy for breast cancer and called into the cathedral after a challenging bout of treatment.

Out of nowhere, a beautifully formed, perfect white feather caught her attention from just below the intricate cathedral ceiling. It elegantly spiralled downwards, landing in the palm of her hand with perfect grace and precision. With it, it brought a sense of peacefulness, reassurance and love. At that moment, my friend was struck by the unquestionable knowledge that she would overcome her disease. She was also convinced that she had celestial help on her side.

My friend wasn't sure if the feather was a sign from her brother-in-law who had passed four years earlier, or if it was a gift from an angel. But she did know that it was definitely a sign from the heavens and a response to her prayers for everything to be okay. And indeed, two years on, she is the picture of robust health and her illness is little more than a distant memory.

Coins too, must be a relatively easy thing to apport, as numerous people have told me of spontaneously appearing coins, particularly in the period immediately after a loved one's death. The coins are commonly of the same denomination, so that the consistency of their appearance cannot be dismissed as coincidental.

A gentleman named Marcus told me that in the two years since his father's death, he has repeatedly been showered with gifts of coins. The coins appear in the most unlikely of places, with a particular favourite location being Marcus's shoes!

"And he does the feather thing too," laughed Marcus. "He drops them in our hair when we're watching TV... we end up looking like American Indians!"

Marcus and his family always acknowledge these spirit gifts and make sure to say thank you whenever they appear. Marcus goes so far as to take photos, as he says, "You never know when this is going to stop."

I told Marcus that I didn't expect the phenomena to cease any time soon, as by acknowledging his father's presence, he was encouraging him to manifest all the more. I have often said that attention is the greatest gift we can give our deceased loved ones, as they thrive on knowing that their messages are getting through.

Other people still, report significant songs playing repeatedly on the radio. Possibly through energetically affecting the transmission of radio waves, the spirits are able to play us the songs we associate with them, thereby making sure that they are in our thoughts.

Many of my friends have reported this phenomenon, and indeed it has also happened to me.

I was heading home after a night spent out of town where I had been the guest at a well-known medium's séance. My friend, Deni, had come through most strongly, identifying himself both by name and his date of birth. Deni gave us enough information for me to be convinced of his presence, but it seemed he was keen to validate his presence all the more.

As I turned on the radio for the journey home, the first song to belt out of the car stereo was Deni's funeral song. Of course the radio had somehow turned itself up to full volume! It was an obscure, raucous song which was most inappropriate for a funeral, but it summed Deni up perfectly. Hearing it now made me laugh out loud, and being able to laugh at it made me appreciate how much I'd healed since his passing.

I thanked Deni for the gift he had given me, not only in that particular moment, but also at the séance the previous evening. Knowing he was still the same funny, mischievous friend he had been in life filled my heart with joy.

My sister, Vlasta, had a similar experience with her car radio, but hers involved the family pet!

Vlasta's family dog, Clyde, had been suffering from heart disease for several months, his state of health rapidly deteriorating to the point where he could hardly breathe. The family had no choice but to have their beloved dog put to sleep.

The night before he passed away, Vlasta spent the night cradling the little Shih Tzu in her arms. It was her son, Josh's birthday, and they had held off having Clyde put to rest that day as they didn't want Josh to forever associate his birthday with his beloved pet's death.

Poor Clyde was struggling to breathe and was clearly agitated; the only time he would be calm was when Vlasta was singing. Despite feeling thoroughly crushed herself, she managed to soothe Clyde with her repetitive rendition of an old Bee Gees song fittingly titled, *How Can You Mend a Broken Heart?* It seemed to echo Clyde's physical state as well as Vlasta's emotional one.

So with Clyde bundled up in a blanket in her arms, she sang through the night until he managed to drop into a fitful sleep.

The following morning, Vlasta and her eldest son, Nick, took the old dog to the veterinary hospital to be put down. The rest of the family were too distraught to attend, and indeed, it was a harrowing and heart-breaking visit.

Vlasta was too upset to go to work the following day and decided to allow herself the day off to grieve. Rather than wasting the entire day, she decided she would try to keep busy and resolved to hire a carpet cleaner and make a start on cleaning the rugs.

She drove to the local shopping centre to hire the steam cleaner and was surprised at how difficult she found it to hold herself together. Acting normal was a struggle; life just didn't feel the same without Clyde.

She returned to the car on the brink of tears. As she turned on the radio, the torrent of tears she'd been suppressing burst forth. The opening strains of *How Can You Mend a Broken Heart?* came playing through the car stereo system. She couldn't help but think it was a sign from Clyde.

Vlasta and Clyde

As she cried and sang along, Vlasta felt as though Clyde was watching. A happier, healthier puppy dog version of her beloved pet who had died.

Stories such as those which have graced this chapter are comforting reminders of the eternal nature of the soul. Our spirit family, both human and animal, remain connected to us irrespective of death. It's a heartening thought and even more precious when we are sensitive enough to pick up on these visitations ourselves.

Although many of us have long-accepted that our departed family members still walk beside us, not so many are convinced that our deceased pets continue to do so too. Take it from me (and from the countless others who report after-death visits from pets); the souls of our pets survive death too.

Most of my family have been lucky enough to see our deceased cat, Willow, darting down our passageway. She is little more than a fleeting shadow, but vivid enough for us to know she is happily inhabiting her new spirit body. I have also felt the gentle pressure of her paws kneading the quilt on my bed so palpably that I have turned on the light to check if it was one of our living cats. Of course, there was no cat to be seen.

Spirit visitations from those we love, whether they are man or beast, are more common that we may think. It's just that they can be extremely fleeting and subtle, so we need to pique our awareness and allow the signs to start filtering in. As I've said so many times before, if you do receive a sign, be sure to offer thanks and acknowledgement. It may just be the most gratefully-received gift you will ever give!

Chapter Six

Neighbourly Secrets

In the wake of the preceding uplifting stories, I think it's prudent to remember that interactions with the spirit world are not always sweetness and light.

Although I've never experienced a negative manifestation whilst conducting a séance, there have been occasions where the spirits have revealed information which would have been better left unsaid. This chapter serves as a warning–if you do choose to make contact with spirits, you may be on the receiving end of more information than you bargained for...

I was contacted by a local property manager, who told me that the tenants of one of her rental properties were complaining that their house was haunted. She wondered if I would be able to help.

It seemed that the household was being targeted by a poltergeist. The couple frequently returned home from work to find their drawers opened and in disarray. The laundry basket was often upturned, its contents strewn across the room. At first glance it appeared as though the home had been broken into, but there were no signs of forced entry and nothing was missing.

The manifestations became steadily more frequent, until eventually it seemed as though something untoward was happening every day. In addition to the drawers and laundry being interfered with, the woman often felt an unseen presence climb into bed with her. This was particularly unnerving, as her husband slept on the other side of the house so that his snoring didn't disturb her.

I made my way to their two-storey townhouse on a wintery Monday night. I was greeted by the husband, Dave, who stood at the front door drinking red wine from a crystal goblet. He simultaneously puffed on a fat cigar, wafting its smoke towards me as I followed him down the hallway.

When conducting séances, I generally advise my sitters to abstain from alcohol beforehand, lest it lower their vibration. Keeping the vibration high lessens the chance of attracting negative, earthbound entities. Also, being affected by alcohol increases the likelihood of an opportunistic ghost attaching itself to you. They may do so for many reasons, one of which may be wanting to vicariously enjoy the effects of alcohol through the intoxicated sitter.

As Dave led me out to the back patio area, he introduced me to his wife, Lara, and their next door neighbour, Denise. Both ladies sat sipping wine as they smoked their cigarettes, possibly trying to stifle their nerves. After exchanging pleasantries, I asked if I could do a walk-through of the house. I wanted to see if I could pick up on any presences and to gauge which room would be the best in which to conduct the séance.

The house was pervaded by a dense, oppressive energy that seemed to intensify as I approached the stairwell. I glanced up to see a diminutive figure perched halfway up the stairs, and it darted to the first floor landing when I addressed it.

Feeling just a little nervous, I slowly made my way up the stairs. The entire first floor was just one big room. It seemed as though it was mostly used for storage, although there was a small area set up as office space and a shrine area which paid homage to Dave's Rosicrucian faith. I stood at the top of the stairs rather than venturing into the darkness.

"Hello!" I called out. "Would anyone like to show themselves in my photo?"

I took a quick snap which captured a small orb against the far wall.

"Would you like to speak with us?" I asked.

Another flash of light suggested that the answer was yes.

"Okay," I said. "Give me a minute and I'll be back. I'll just go downstairs and get the others."

I made my way to the group out the back and told them that we would be holding the séance upstairs.

Moments later we were seated around my spirit contact table with white candles lit and our hands poised over its shiny surface. It didn't take long for the first spirit to come through, after which the messages barrelled in one after another.

The first spirit introduced herself as Frances and told us that it was she who had been sitting on the stairs. Frances told us that she was eight years of age. She confessed to rummaging through the drawers and laundry, but pointed out that she hadn't been doing so alone.

"Who else has been doing it?" I asked

FRED.

"Okay... we'll get to Fred in a minute, but first I want to speak with you. Have you been trying to frighten Dave and Lara?"

NO.

"So why have you been going through their things? Are you just trying to get their attention?"

YES.

"Why?" I asked.

The planchette skimmed across the table.

PROTECT LARA.

"Protect Lara from whom?"

GRAHAM!

By now, Lara was looking ashen.

"Does this make sense to you?" I asked her.

Lara nodded.

"So who's Graham?"

At this point, Dave interjected, and told me that Graham was his best friend.

The planchette continued to move frenetically, without our prompting.

GET RID OF GRAHAM. GRAHAM EVIL.

"Whoa!" I said. "I don't think Graham is evil... it's probably just that you don't like him. Tell me why you have a problem with him."

GRAHAM HURT LARA. FRANCES LOVES LARA. HATE GRAHAM.

Visibly affected by the communication, Lara decided to come clean. She told us that Graham (who was a frequent house guest) had often made moves on her, sneaking into her bedroom when Dave was asleep. On one occasion he walked into Lara's room stark naked, pretending he had confused Lara's bedroom with his own.

Dave was not as surprised as Lara expected him to be, and he went on to tell us about some of his own exchanges with Graham.

"He said that he could have Lara with a snap of his fingers," said Dave. "He was drunk at the time, so I took it with a grain of salt. I just presumed it was the alcohol talking."

"Well, I can't stand him," said Lara. "It's not just the way he is with me, it's everything about him. There's something really dark about him..."

Returning our attention to Frances, I asked her if Graham posed a risk to Lara, other than threatening to invade her bed. Frances responded without hesitation, telling us that Graham was determined to destroy the couple's relationship. His jealousy of Dave was almost pathological, despite supposedly being his best friend. Alarmingly, Frances also warned that Graham had a violent side, and if he didn't get what he wanted, it was likely to come to light.

"Is that why you've been trying to get Dave and Lara's attention?" I asked.

YES, responded Frances. KEEP GRAHAM OUT. KEEP LARA SAFE.

Frances told us that Fred was trying to keep Lara safe too, and that was the reason he'd been regularly jumping into her bed.

"May we speak to Fred?" I asked.

After a little persuasion, young Frances agreed to step back and allow the other spirit to come through.

He introduced himself as Fred Byers, the revelation of which sent gasps around the table.

"Do you know him?" I asked.

"He's the guy who built the first houses on the street in the 1800s. That's why it's called Byers Street!"

The couple told me that when the paranormal disturbances began, they researched the property and its surrounds. They wanted to establish whether there was anything in its history that could be contributing to the haunting. All they discovered was that Fred Byers had built the first four houses on the street, the first of which was his home. Although it had long since been demolished, it was built on the land where the couple's striking two-storey residence now stood.

As well as being a successful businessman, he also had a reputation as being a well-known womaniser. It could be said that between his property dealings and romantic pursuits, Fred Byers well and truly had his hands full. I wondered whether Fred's womanising ways were continuing beyond the grave.

"Fred, Frances tells us that you've been hopping into bed with Lara... is this true?"

YES.

"Do you like Lara?"

YES.

"Any other reason?" I asked.

KEEP LARA SAFE.

What followed was virtually an identical conversation to the one we had had with Frances. Fred had similarly negative feelings towards Graham and felt that Lara was in danger as long as he was allowed in their home. He admitted to creating the disturbance to get the couple's attention and told us that he and Frances had been united in their attempts to get rid of Graham.

"So what's your connection to Frances?" I asked.

CONNIE'S DAUGHTER, he responded.

"And Connie is...?"

MY LOVER.

"Oh, okay," I said. "But you're not her father?"

NO.

Our conversation continued for quite some time, and we discovered that Frances and Fred's deaths occurred whilst Connie was still alive. Having loved the child as his own, Fred took the young Frances under his wing, and the two had been dwelling together in the astral plane ever since.

When I asked if they needed help to cross over, they were adamant that they were happy as they were. I told them that if they changed their minds to come and seek me out and I would do my best to help them. I also assured them that Lara and Dave would give their warnings due consideration and hopefully oust Graham's negative influence from their lives.

By now, the next-door neighbour was becoming a little impatient and was eager to be on the receiving end of some messages of her own. Prior to the séance commencing, she had confessed to being sceptical. As the evening unfolded, however, she was becoming increasingly open to the reality of spirit communication. Now she wanted to test the spirits out for herself.

"So... do you know me?" she asked.

YES.

"What's my name?"

DENISE.

"What do you know about me?"

BOYFRIEND... RICK.

I looked at Denise for validation, and her awestruck expression confirmed that this was correct. Fred wasted no time in offering insights into Denise and Rick's relationship.

PROBLEMS... RICK TOO YOUNG.

I asked Fred if he knew how old Rick was, to which he responded 25. Given that Denise was well into her forties, I could understand why problems were beginning to surface between them.

RICK SCARED.

"Of what?" asked Denise, beginning to feel exasperated. "What's he got to be scared of?"

COMMITMENT, spelt Fred.

By now, Denise was beginning to wonder whether Fred's insights were based on what he had actually observed, or if he was just jumping to obvious conclusions given her and Rick's age gap.

"So how do I know that you actually know us and what's happening in our relationship? How do I know you're not just guessing?"

Denise's questioning set the planchette streaking across the table, with information too intimate to repeat. Needless to say, Fred had no qualms about revealing intensely personal details about Denise and Rick's relationship. He went so far as to report on their sex life, the accurate details of which could not have been a fluke.

Denise flushed bright red and began shaking.

"Mr Byers!" she gasped. "I would have thought that a gentleman of your era would exercise some respect and discretion! What you've been doing is wrong! How dare you watch us in bed together?"

At this point, everyone was getting a little hot under the collar.

"And I suppose you watch me and Lara having sex too?" said Dave indignantly.

NO... ONLY DENISE.

"Why just me?" asked Denise.

Since it's X-rated, Fred's answer cannot be repeated. I will, however, say that Fred's preference for watching

Denise's bedroom antics was because of a particularly risqué practice she often engaged in. By comparison, Fred found Dave and Lara's sex-life boring. Upon this revelation, Dave felt affronted all the more!

Since the tone of the séance had started to degenerate, I thought it best to ask the spirits to step back and close down the table. We finished off by taking a few photos, and Fred and Frances were happy to appear as pale, luminescent orbs.

Debriefing afterwards, Denise admitted she hadn't expected such incredible and disturbing proof that spirit communication is possible. She wondered how she could ever have sex again, knowing that Fred Byers was likely to be observing from the dark recesses of her bedroom.

"I suppose you can just ask him to leave," I suggested. "Spirits are generally respectful of our wishes. You may need to be quite forceful though..."

"But how will I know whether he's still there?" she asked.

"Ummm... you won't. You've just got to put it out of your head I guess. Or just give up on the idea of having sex ever again."

I could see Denise's mind ticking over, wondering how she was ever going to rid herself of her invisible peeping Tom. I felt sorry for her, especially since such intimate sexual secrets had been revealed in front of her neighbours and a complete stranger.

"So how about you guys?" I asked Dave and Lara. "What are you going to do about Graham?"

Lara was adamant that Graham would not be coming into their home again. It's what she'd been wanting for months. Dave, on the other hand, was surprisingly hesitant to cast Graham aside.

"He's the only friend I've made since moving from the UK," he said. "And he hasn't got anyone else either... we're best mates."

I was surprised that he would consider a man who is trying to steal his wife as his best mate and suggested that maybe he needed to forge some new friendships. He was putting up with shoddy treatment for all the wrong reasons. If what Frances and Fred said was true, Graham wouldn't stop until he either had Lara to himself, or destroyed Lara and Dave's relationship. Or worse. The spirits seemed to think that Lara's safety was at risk.

By the time I left that evening, Dave had resolved to give serious thought as to whether he would continue his relationship with Graham. In the meantime, he promised Lara that he would not allow him into their home and would only meet up with him in the local pub.

I trust that this will be enough to placate the spirits, and that the laundry basket remains upright and the drawers remain closed. And if they don't, I'm sure Dave knows what he has to do to make sure they do.

As for poor Denise, I hope Fred hasn't affected her relationship with Rick too much. I suspect that even if it's business as usual, she will be conducting her 'business' hidden beneath the sheets!

Chapter Seven

Teenage Terror

Continuing on the topic of mischievous ghosts, teenagers are frequently on the receiving end of ghostly attention. The tumultuous emotions often associated with adolescence are thought to provide a potential energy source for disembodied entities. Ghosts who have lain dormant can suddenly spring into activity as a direct result of the power derived from the blossoming adolescent.

This was certainly the case with regard to my own situation. My teen years saw the resurgence of my clairvoyant abilities, thereby giving rise to regular visitations which absolutely terrified me. The fear that these experiences elicited added further fuel to the ghosts' ever increasing power supply. My unchecked emotions led to a snowball effect that I struggled to suppress. As a result, my family home became the focus of regular poltergeist activity, the memories of which affect me to this day.

Although my teen years are long behind me, I still recall the intensity with which fear dominated my life. A good night's sleep was elusive (if not impossible) and I rarely, if ever, felt safe. As the haunting stretched on, I felt as though I was falling into a void of fear and darkness. Sometimes it felt as though it would be impossible to recover.

Thankfully, I was mistaken. Not only did I emerge from the dark days of the haunting stronger than I was before, but I also learnt some valuable lessons. Negativity begets negativity, whereas being positive allows you to take control. Fear is a powerful emotion which projects itself so strongly that it draws in opportunistic energies. This is almost certainly what happened to me. If I were to live through this type of experience again, I would like to think I would be able to take control and not allow fear to consume me.

My advice to those living through a haunting (particularly children and teenagers) is to firstly understand that the spirit world is rarely malicious. Most manifestations are little more than attention-seeking behaviours—tricks to get your attention and hopefully, a reaction. The best way to cope is to either acknowledge the presence with as little emotion as possible, or to simply tell it to go away. The spirit world is usually very respectful, and whichever spirit is hanging around will generally bow to your wishes. Or at the very least they will refrain from frightening behaviours and revert to being subtle, unassuming presences.

So, in essence, the key is to keep one's fear in check which, of course, is easier said than done. To this end, I have made it my mission to help teens in similar situations to my own, by providing support, understanding and advice. With understanding comes strength, and of course the sooner fear is suppressed, the more quickly the manifestation will subside.

Most of my dealings with teenagers are instigated by their parents who often feel at a loss as to how to help their child. They usually report an increasingly bleak mood pervading the household, with inexplicable phenomena generally being focussed around the adolescent. The teenager often reports a litany of ghost-related events and refuses to sleep on their own. They often sleep on the floor of their parent's bedroom or prefer to sleep in the lounge. Some take up residence with a sibling–they will do anything to avoid being alone.

The range of paranormal manifestations traverses a wide spectrum with some reporting little more than fleeting glimpses of apparitions. Others experience physical phenomena–whereby objects are flung by invisible hands, they are physically touched, or they may feel someone sitting on the bed. Depending on one's resilience, all have the potential to be extremely frightening.

In fourteen-year-old Max's case, he was regularly assailed by the vision of two glowing red eyes. The eyes would suddenly appear in the middle of his bedroom and hover before him for several minutes. As one would expect, he was absolutely terrified. Max also reported that sudden putrid smells regularly wafted into his room. Again, the manifestation lasted for long enough for him to know that he had not imagined it.

On occasion, Max would hear someone calling out his name, the masculine voice sounding gruff and impatient.

Max reached the point where he put off going to sleep until later and later, and when he finally did, it would be in a sleeping bag near his mother's bedroom. He kept a pedestal fan running right beside him, hoping that its soothing whir would drown out any ghostly voices and lull him to sleep.

Things came to a head when he awoke after an afternoon nap to see a hazy apparition leaning over him. It seemed to be patting his hair. Understandably, Max was sent into a blind panic. He couldn't even feel safe when he was sleeping!

His mother rang me in despair.

It seemed that we were dealing with two separate entities—the foul-smelling, red-eyed presence and a protective, gentle one. Researching the home's history revealed that it had been the long-time home of an old widower. He had lived in the house for over twenty years.

Max had indeed fleetingly seen the apparition of a stooped old man. Although not the evil presence he was trying to portray, he was certainly grumpy and wanted Max and his family out. Being an impressionable teenager singled Max out as the obvious target, and his escalating fear made him an increasingly attractive one.

Whilst the old man was hell-bent on trying to scare off Max and his family so that he could reclaim his house, there was an opposing, positive energy that was trying to offer comfort. The hair-patting apparition could have either been Max's spirit guide, or perhaps even more likely, the spirit of a deceased relative. The positivity it was radiating was no doubt trying to counteract the old man's bullying presence. Nevertheless, young Max found both apparitions similarly frightening, and it was this spirit's visitation that prompted Max's mother to call me.

The first objective was to convince the old man that he was dead. He had to understand that he no longer belonged in the house. To this end, we smudged the house—a process by which white sage is burnt and wafted into every corner of every room, whilst addressing the earthbound spirit.

We firmly told him that he needed to move on, all the while treating him with respect and compassion. We told him that he had to leave Max alone, that it was time to move into the light. We also invited positive, loving energies to draw in all around us, so that negative energy was replaced with positivity in the home. At the same time, I wasn't trying to move on any protective family spirits, as I knew that their subtle influences would help keep Max balanced, comforted and safe.

The difference in the home's energy was immediately apparent, although Max's mother believes that the old fellow still calls in from time to time to check up on his beloved home. I would like to think that he is calling in as a crossed over spirit and that he has left his earthly, bullying ways behind him.

"I tell him to move on anyway," laughed Max's mother. "Now that Max is happily back in his room, I'm not taking any chances!"

I have recently spoken to Max's family, and overall, he's doing pretty well. Although thinking about his past experiences does sometimes scare him, he knows enough to avoid succumbing to his old fears. I suspect that Max may well be a budding clairvoyant, so he will always attract his fair share of ghostly hangers on. His mother, Gretch, also sensitive, is mindful of ghostly attachments and tries to keep her home's vibration high. She also takes Max for regular Reiki and healing sessions, which seem to be working wonders.

Fourteen-year-old Max overcame the undesirable attentions of ghosts with the help of healing sessions and

Reiki. Smudging the family home also proved to be of great help.

Disturbances amongst teenagers are more prevalent than is commonly believed, particularly when the teenager possesses mediumistic abilities like Max. I encountered a similar scenario with a young man named Mitchell, who is the son of my childhood friend, May.

May called me in distress. Her son was becoming a nervous wreck as the result of a ghost taking up residence in his bedroom. At fifteen years of age and with blossoming clairvoyance, Mitch had caught the attentions of a disembodied 'someone' who was refusing to go away.

Although he spent time in his bedroom during the day, the evenings were another matter altogether. Sleeping in his bedroom was out of the question. Mitchell much preferred the discomfort of sleeping on his parents' bedroom floor. Being at home by himself was also not an option, even in the middle of the day.

Since she hadn't felt anything negative in the house herself, May wasn't sure how to deal with her son's all-consuming anxiety. Mitchell's fearfulness was steadily escalating, and it had reached the point where it was detrimentally affecting his sense of well-being. May called me in desperation and asked if I could help. By the time I called around to investigate, it had been going on for months.

Armed with my smudge-stick and pendulum, I did an initial walk-through of the house. I certainly didn't feel anything ominous.

My pendulum is a useful backup when planning on communicating with spirits, as my clairaudience is notoriously unreliable. I'm predominantly clairvoyant, which means that seeing spirits is my forte. My clairaudience–the ability to hear spirits–is nowhere near as developed, which can lead to many frustrating spirit encounters.

In light of this, I often use a pendulum when I know that spirits are near. The pendulum works by channelling energy and allows us to communicate with either disembodied entities or our higher selves. Although the answers are limited to yes, no or maybe, with clear and appropriate questioning it can be a useful tool.

I wasn't sure if I'd need the smudge stick, but had brought it along just in case. A smudge stick is simply a bundle of dried sage, which is burnt when doing house cleansing. Its pungent smoke is wafted into the corners of every room whilst simultaneously encouraging earthbound energies to leave. I use the smudge stick whenever I encounter ghosts who are reluctant to move on–it's part of my armoury when working to resolve hauntings. In most cases, though, I find it isn't necessary. With compassion and encouragement, most ghosts can be convinced that crossing into the light is a good idea.

May and I sat at the dining table chatting, so that I could take time to gauge the house's energy more accurately. That's when it started—the parade of flashing lights. I grabbed my camera and started snapping, but there were no orbs to be seen.

Of course, as soon as I put the camera down, the lights resumed going berserk. It was as if they were playing a game with me. At the very least, I knew they were trying to get my attention.

I decided to do a brief meditation to better tune in to whoever was around. May and I joined hands across the table, allowing our energy to merge and heighten. This would hopefully raise our vibration enough to connect with the spirit energy around us.

It wasn't long before a gentleman came through. A pleasant, unassuming energy who introduced himself as John. To identify spirits when I only have a pendulum, I ask for their name and then slowly go through the alphabet. The pendulum starts swinging when I call out the correct letter. This is repeated until the spirit's entire name is spelt out — it's time-consuming and far from ideal, but a useful tool to fall back on when a yes or no answer doesn't suffice.

May told me that John had been their next door neighbour and that he had died several years ago. John was accompanied by his wife, Evie, who had passed away a couple of years later. It seems he had been waiting for her and had therefore chosen not to cross over until Evie, too, was ready. But now, they were both earthbound, as Evie was refusing to go into the light.

We spoke to John first.

"Did you see the light when you first passed away?" I asked him.

YES, he replied

"Can you see it now?"

NO...

John said that he wanted to cross over, but couldn't find the light. He was well and truly stuck and unsure as to how to move on. But there was another pressing problem that John was having trouble overcoming. Evie was adamant that she would not be moving on. It seemed she preferred to remain on the earth plane. She wanted to stay in an environment that felt familiar and safe.

I asked Evie to step forward, and she confirmed what John had told us. She wasn't going anywhere! She too, had seen the light upon her death, but was too frightened to move towards it. It felt much safer staying put in the old neighbourhood, and she felt particularly at home in her young friend, Mitchell's room.

"You do realise that you're scaring him, don't you?" I asked.

I approached the matter with as much diplomacy as I could muster, as I didn't want to upset her. I knew that Evie was a good person and that scaring Mitchell was most certainly not her intention. But I needed her to know that her energy was adversely affecting him and that he wouldn't be able to feel comfortable in his bedroom until she moved on.

She seemed to be taking it all in, and kept repeating *YES* to confirm that she understood.

"So are you ready to cross?" I asked.

She responded with a small, unconvincing *YES*.

"Evie?" I asked again. "Will you cross now?"

NO!

May and I looked at each other and sighed. Why had I thought that this was going to be easy?

I went into my usual spiel which I use when I'm trying to cross spirits over. I began by asking Evie if she was scared. The pendulum began to swing in large, purposeful circles, clearly indicating that she was. She was also worried about never being able to see her loved ones again, especially her children. She thought that crossing over meant she would never be able to come back, so she had chosen to remain on the earth plane instead.

"Oh, Evie!" I said. "Of course you can still come back and check on your family. Some spirits even go on to become spirit guides... you could keep an eye on them every day! But you have to cross first; you need to transition into spirit."

I lowered my voice.

"And Evie... you don't really want to be a ghost, do you? Because that's what you are now and will continue to be until you cross over. That's why Mitchell finds you so scary... your energy is too heavy."

I told Evie of all the love, comfort and healing that awaited her in the light. I reminded her that her family who had passed before her were all there waiting. The pendulum swung more and more powerfully; consistently indicating *YES*.

"So you're ready to go now?" I asked. And again, another undeniable *YES!* John of course was ready and waiting, so I asked if they could see the light.

The pendulum swung to *NO*.

It was time to move into phase B.

May and I joined hands once again, and I talked May through a simple guided meditation. Together we managed to flood the room with an intense and brilliant light, which we then focussed into a corner of the room. I felt as though my whole being was pulsating and my cheeks began to burn. Surely this was doing something!

"Can you see the beautiful light?" I asked.

Evie responded *YES!*

I told her that it was filled with love for her and she needn't fear going into it. I asked her to allow herself to drift towards the beautiful feelings which were radiating from the light.

At this point, May's parents, who died over thirty years ago, stepped forward to help. They had very much transitioned into spirit and were going to help John and Evie on their way. Although May's parents were a regular presence in her home, as crossed-over spirits they were able to come and go. They had assumed roles of guardianship over May's family and drew in close whenever they were needed. They were a wonderful example for John and Evie to follow, as they were proof of the ongoing bonds between the living and the dead.

"So you're going then?" I asked.

YES!

"You're sure now?" I teased.

YES!

The pendulum went completely still as if unseen hands had suddenly arrested it, and just like that, they were gone.

"Evie?" I asked.

Nothing. It seemed that the happy foursome had already transitioned into the light.

I looked at May who obviously felt as emotional as I did. We smiled at each other as we took it all in.

"They've gone, haven't they?" she said, her eyes brimming with tears.

"For now, they have." I said. "But I'd bet my life on the fact that they'll be back!"

I told May that she should tell Mitchell about the events of the morning and explain that it was Evie and John in his bedroom all along. Although he would no doubt find the concept a little unsettling, he had shared a close bond with them when they were alive and would understand why they had chosen to stay around him.

"And when they do visit again, it will be as spirits, not as ghosts. Mitch will feel their energy completely differently."

I explained that when the dead remain earthbound, their energy is low vibrational and dense. To a sensitive like Mitchell, this can feel negative and oppressive. It was this negative energy which was repelling him from his bedroom. These non-crossed over souls are ghosts, and may or may not take things to the next level and generate a haunting.

Spirits, however, are transitioned souls like May's parents. They are high vibrational, positive energies and generally leave a sense of well-being in their wake. So when Evie and John come to call in the future, they will manifest completely differently than they did as ghosts.

My smudge stick went unused that morning, and I stuffed it back into my handbag.

"I would've felt wrong using this," I said to May. "It would've felt as though I was moving them on without their blessing. I'm much happier having talked them round."

May agreed. As in most instances of dealing with ghosts, they are earthbound for a reason. Fear of the unknown is the most common motive for failing to progress to the higher spirit realms, or in some instances, ghosts may hang around due to a desire to address unfinished business. In some cases, the deceased may not have fully grasped that they are dead and may linger in a twilight state until they can absorb the fact that they are no longer living.

To help these souls transition, their particular reason for remaining amongst the living needs to be addressed. Once their concerns, fears and confusion can be allayed, they are usually grateful to have the opportunity to move on. A loving, kind approach works wonders.

Ghosts are rarely the sinister entities we sometimes imagine them to be. They are usually just misplaced souls needing guidance and love. Or sometimes they are simply the spirits of our departed loved ones, trying to let us know that they are still a part of our lives.

Such was the case with another young teenager who approached me for help with an apparent haunting. I met Casey whilst conducting a spirit contact evening at my local hotel.

Thirteen-year-old Casey found herself on the receiving end of frequent paranormal phenomena. Her blossoming clairvoyance proved to be a beacon for restless ghosts.

The Kalamunda Hotel is 105 years old and has a widespread reputation for being haunted. It took me a while to actually make the time to go there, and when I finally did, I was overwhelmed by its generous population of ghosts.

After picking up on the hotel's numerous ghostly inhabitants, I decided to try and connect with them. My meeting with Preshti had increased my confidence, and I felt compelled to do my best to help them cross over. In order to do so, I arranged for a group of thirty like-minded people to attend a gathering at the hotel to initiate contact with the ghosts and help them move on. I reasoned that the combined energy of thirty people would go a long way towards achieving our common goal.

The group was mostly recruited from my Facebook page, with a few close friends and family members thrown in for good measure. We gathered in the upstairs Dome Room—named in recognition of the stunning stained glass dome which dominated its high ceiling. The meeting was set to begin at 7 p.m.

Whilst waiting for the last few stragglers, I noticed an anxious-looking young girl sitting next to a woman I presumed was her mother.

"Hello sweetheart!" I said. "Are you looking forward to tonight? My daughter will be fuming when I tell her we had someone around her age here... she was desperate to come!"

The girl smiled nervously and looked towards her mother. She told me that her name was Casey and that she was thirteen.

"Well, there you go," I laughed. "My daughter's not quite twelve, so she'll just have to be patient for another year!"

Well aware of the young girl's apprehension, I asked her if she felt scared.

"No," she said. "I've been really looking forward to it..."

I didn't entirely believe that Casey was as relaxed about proceedings as she said she was, and as the night unfolded, the reason for her attendance soon became clear.

It transpired that Casey had been on the receiving end of a gamut of ghostly visits, to the point where she was too frightened to sleep in her own bedroom. It all began to sound frighteningly familiar.

"There's constant banging and strange noises," said her mother. "It's really starting to take over our lives. And it all seems to be concentrated around Casey."

Casey said that she was aware of a constant presence in her bedroom. Not wanting to give too much away, she asked if we could possibly contact the persistent spirit and find out exactly who it was.

Although the manifestations were quite strong, they were generally benign. Recently, however, it seemed as though they were escalating.

"I just pull the covers over my head and wait for whoever it is to go away, but it's really freaking me out. They're making me feel petrified!"

Obviously mature for her age and well versed in matters related to the paranormal, Casey told me that she was concerned about what would happen now that she was approaching puberty.

"I'm just scared that the ghosts are going to get stronger," she said with a quiver in her voice.

Casey knew full well that ghosts thrive on the latent energy of blossoming teenagers, and in particular the emotional energy supplied by teenage girls. She knew that her demographic was particularly prone to poltergeists and the thought of it terrified her.

Casey went on to describe a constant, masculine presence, which most often manifested in a particular corner of her bedroom.

"Can you actually see him?" I asked.

"Yes," she said, her fear now palpable. "He just looks like a black shadow..."

Casey reluctantly shared her most frightening experience. She felt that discussing the events of that particular evening made them feel even more terrifying and real. Giving the ghosts attention seemed to somehow empower them, and she was worried about doing anything that could possibly rile them up.

"The scariest night was just a few months ago," said Casey. "Towards the end of the summer."

"It felt as though my whole room was somehow pulsating. When I put my hand up onto the window, the glass felt as cold as ice... and the glass was vibrating. I just bolted out of there and went and slept with mum!"

"Well, someone's obviously trying to get your attention," I said.

I tried to play it down so as not to scare her, but I couldn't ignore the hollow feeling of fear which had suddenly crept into my stomach. I remembered all too well my own teenage experiences with poltergeists and was mortified to think that this sweet girl before me could be heading down that same path.

There was nothing else for it than to sit at my spirit contact table and see if someone was waiting to come through. Perhaps it was just a case of harmless, attention-seeking behaviour on the part of the spirits. If that was the case, the best way to placate them was to give them some attention.

Since I was feeling drained after conducting the group séance, my friend, Jacqui, stepped in to facilitate the spirit contact.

Casey moved in nervously as she took her place at the table. Her mother and her grandmother also assumed their positions, showering young Casey with as much love and support as they could muster.

It wasn't long before a strong spirit began to come through.

When the spirit announced his name, young Casey began to cry.

"It's only Granddad!" soothed her mother. "He's just been trying to let you know that he's still around... I bet you he's been looking out for you all along!"

Casey's mother was quickly proven to be correct, as the messages from her father confirmed what she'd just said.

He had indeed been creating a ruckus in the household, but only because Casey had been ignoring him. He was well aware of Casey's clairvoyance and couldn't understand why he wasn't getting through. As a result, he was manifesting more and more strongly, ever hopeful that his beloved granddaughter would finally acknowledge him.

By now, young Casey was reduced to tears.

"I do love you," she said, quietly addressing the table. "But it's just that you're scaring me. I know you don't mean to, but I can't help feeling scared..."

I told Casey that now that her grandfather had her attention, he would be happy to step back.

"All he wanted was for you to know that he's there," I said.

I was very mindful of the fact that Casey's clairvoyance would be acting as a beacon to spirit energy. So not only would her grandfather be drawn to her, but she would be attracting all manner of wayward spirit energies too. I knew this first hand from when I was Casey's age. I suspect that Casey's grandfather was also aware of this and had thus taken on the role as her gate-keeper. He wanted to ensure that no negative energies could get through.

Speaking to Casey instantly took me back to my own experiences as a teenager, and my heart went out to her. I hoped that with such a strong support network around her (coupled with a wisdom and maturity well beyond her years) Casey would be able to avoid the poltergeist dramas which had dominated my life as a teen.

"You're just like I was when I was a girl," I said as I hugged her before she left. "Except, of course, you're much prettier!"

"And..." I stressed. "The best part is that you know exactly what's going on. When I was in the thick of it, I had no idea what was happening! I just thought that I was living in a haunted house! Remember, you're the one with the power, and if you're not in the mood for visitors, just tell them to go away!"

"But what about Granddad?" Casey asked quietly. "Won't he get upset?"

"Not at all," I assured her. "Your grandfather loves you. That's the whole reason he's here. He'd be mortified if he thought he was scaring you. He just wants you to know he's got you covered!"

I assured Casey that her grandfather would probably be a more subtle presence from now on. He had achieved his aim by letting her know he was protecting her, so there'd be no need to keep asserting his presence so strongly.

"But if you do get freaked out by anything, all you need to do is call me. Remember that I've been there too, so I can completely relate."

Casey took my card with a smile.

"I'm feeling better about this already!" she said.

As she left the hotel that evening, I just knew that Casey had already turned the corner. Fear is fuelled by the unknown, but now Casey was armed with the facts. And dispensing with her intense fear would rob any mischievous entities of a potential power source. Together with her grandfather's unwavering protection, Casey was unlikely to go wrong. I was grateful that she had been averted from travelling the same harrowing path as my own.

The medium's life is not easy, but knowing that there are loving spirits on your side certainly makes a difference. Even if they do have the occasional propensity for freaking you out!

I have often said that there is so much more good than evil in the world, and the same holds true for ghosts.

Even when ghostly displays seem frightening and confronting, in most instances this type of manifestation is borne from the spirit's own fear. So before you start brandishing crosses and sprinkling holy water, take the time to try and connect with your resident ghost. More often than not, they will be grateful for the attention. If you are not particularly sensitive to spirit energy, you may need to call in a medium to facilitate contact. It will be well worth the effort.

Always remember that ghosts are fundamentally no different to you or me, except for the fact that they have discarded their outer shell. One day you may find yourself in the same predicament as they are in now—in need of a compassionate person to help you cross over. You can be that compassionate person now.

As Max, Mitchell and Casey's stories indicate, teenagers can certainly act as beacons for paranormal activity, and indeed, these three examples are just three of many teenager-focussed episodes I have come across.

Other teenagers who have shared their stories with me report a wide variety of manifestations. Some are as innocuous as seeing a shampoo bottle 'walk' across the top of a shower rail, or a computer may suddenly turn itself on. Others report visits which come across as slightly more confronting, such as scratching noises coming from inside wardrobes and walls, or feeling an invisible someone beside them in the bed. Some have spoken of doors and cupboards opening of their own accord.

Regardless of where one's experiences fall within this spectrum, the approach towards managing them is always the same. The ghosts need to be moved on and normality within the teenager's life needs to be restored. Remaining spiritually strong is crucial, and I wish I had known this when I was going through my own teen years.

These days, people are much more informed about spiritual matters, and help in situations such as these is always at hand. Most importantly, it's comforting to remind oneself that you are not alone, even though living through a haunting sometimes feels like the loneliest experience in the world. I encourage those who are going through this type of experience to talk to friends and family, to read about similar experiences to your own and to empower yourself with knowledge. Most of all, remind yourself that not all spirits are scary, and that you have a faithful guide of your own (or several) by your side. So when your guide or a deceased loved one strokes you on the head (as Max's did to him), try not to freak out. It's just a loving reminder that you are never alone and that any mischievous entities are going to have a tough time getting through!

Chapter Eight

The Lure of the Ouija

It's the subject of countless horror stories and has proven to be the downfall of many an inexperienced dabbler, yet the Ouija board still can't shake off its irresistible allure. Despite its well-known reputation for creating paranormal havoc, the board continues to be used by countless would-be mediums throughout the world.

The purists brand it as evil, going so far as to suggest that it may inadvertently summon the devil. Others suggest that it is little more than an expression of the subconscious, whereby the glass or planchette is merely being moved by the sitter's higher self. Another school of thought is that the spirits who manifest through the board are low vibrational entities—quite often mischievous souls who are functioning on the astral plane. As such, it's considered unwise to invite these unevolved energies into one's home.

The Ouija board has a justifiably chequered reputation.

Most people have a Ouija horror story, whether it be their own or that of a friend. It's surprising that despite its bad rap, people are still drawn to experimenting with it, quite often with potentially devastating results.

An acquaintance of mine (whom I shall refer to as Maureen) approached me to ask my opinion about Ouija boards. Had she asked me twelve months earlier, my response would have been entirely different. These days, however, I feel I have a more grounded attitude, based on personal experience rather than urban myths and rumours.

It is of course true that opening doors to other dimensions is fraught with danger and possible risks; however, this is as true for Ouija boards as it is for tarot cards, crystal balls or any other divining device. Any paranormal tool is used by inviting spirit energy to manifest, so of course each invitation needs to be extended with appropriate preparation and with protection firmly in place.

In the past, I have likened indiscriminate Ouija use with opening one's front door and inviting all and sundry into one's home. This is exactly what those who sit at the board and begin proceedings by asking, *Is anyone there?* are doing. They're inviting strange and possibly destructive energies into their environment. And just as an unsavoury person may compromise your personal safety, so too can a disgruntled earthbound spirit with mischief on its mind.

The board itself, however, is by no means evil, despite its reputation to the contrary. I have even heard some people claim that the only way to safely dispose of a Ouija board is to burn it. Adding further fuel to its chequered reputation is the belief that when the board is burnt, its destruction is accompanied by the sound of unearthly screams. This I cannot help but dismiss as outrageously far-fetched!

The truth of the matter is that yes, the board can be used as a portal by negative, opportunistic energies, but only if it is used indiscriminately by inexperienced hands. If it is used with respect by someone with an appropriately high vibration, it can be just another vehicle to allow loving energies to come through.

That said, Maureen had already formed her own opinion with regard to Ouija, which she had gleaned purely from her own personal experiences. She just wanted my take on what she considered to be a potentially destructive tool.

"The problem for me was that I became addicted to it," she said. "And that's pretty scary when you consider that I started using it when I was thirteen!"

Maureen didn't keep her Ouija use a secret and revelled in astounding her friends with some of the amazing information she received through the board. She didn't even keep the details of her new hobby from the school nuns, who warned her that she was flirting with extreme danger. They insisted that she stop immediately, lest an evil spirit, or indeed the devil himself, tried to commandeer her soul.

Maureen paid little heed to their warnings; she was enjoying herself too much to consider the possibility of stopping. Even as she relays her stories now, there is an unmistakable glimmer of excitement in her eyes.

"I just learnt so much from them," she said, referring to the spirits. "It felt like I was having my own private history lesson!"

Maureen said that she spoke to numerous deceased relatives and ancestors, and hung onto everything they told her about their lives and the past.

"They also said things about the future," she said. "They weren't always good things either, and sometimes that really frightened me."

It got to the point where Maureen was using the Ouija board almost daily, and as time went on it began to wear her out. She was also starting to feel isolated and depressed. Then one night it all came to a head.

"I was lying in bed when I suddenly began to feel extremely hot, even though it was threatening to snow outside."

"I was woken up by the fact that I was sweating so much, and I found it hard to get back to sleep. It was almost as though I was only just semi-conscious."

Maureen went on to tell me that all of a sudden she was roused by a low and insistent voice–a voice she believed belonged to none other than the devil.

"He told me that it was much cooler outside," said Maureen. "He was encouraging me to climb out of my first story window."

Although she initially resisted, it wasn't long before Maureen started to believe that climbing out of her window was in fact a very good idea. Still in her semi-trance state, the teenage Maureen climbed out of bed and quietly opened the window. A moment later she was enjoying an icy, winter breeze from her perch on the rooftop.

"So there I was," said Maureen, "dressed in nothing more than my baby doll nighty, climbing my way across the roof. It was absurd!"

After navigating her way across the length of the house, Maureen shimmied her way down a rickety drainpipe.

"And that's pretty much when it struck me that something really bizarre was going on."

Finding herself alone and freezing in the frostbitten garden, she went to the front door and rang the bell.

"It would have been about two or three in the morning," she said. "My mum was shocked when she opened the door and saw me!"

When her incredulous mother asked what she was doing, Maureen told her she had climbed out of her window and made her way across the roof.

"Then I just came down the drainpipe," she told her wide-eyed mother, barely able to comprehend having done so herself.

Her mother couldn't understand what would possess Maureen doing something so ridiculously dangerous, and wondered whether she had been sleepwalking.

"It wasn't that, Mum," said Maureen, suddenly feeling frightened. "A voice in my room told me to do it. I think it was the devil!"

Feeling that Maureen's obsessive use of the Ouija board had somehow led to this disturbing disclosure, her mother insisted that the board be destroyed. Although perhaps not entirely believing the devil was responsible for luring her daughter onto the rooftop, she did feel that Maureen's obsessive new hobby and the evening's events were somehow connected. Perhaps a mischievous entity was trying to frighten her by impersonating the devil.

"Whoever it was, scared me into stopping though," she said. "And you know, I must admit that from time to time I still think about it and miss it."

Asked if she was tempted to sit at a Ouija board again, Maureen insisted that she wasn't.

"As exciting as it was, there's no way I could do it again. Especially after that night on the rooftop. I'm a mother now, and I can't afford to take any chances. Imagine if some nasty ghost tried to attach itself to my daughter!"

Maureen's attitude has become guarded and cautious, and rightly so. If she was to revert to dabbling with the board without taking the necessary precautions, who knows what kind of malevolence she could invite into her life? All it would take is a little slip up, and the doors to the lower vibratory dimensions could open and refuse to shut.

But of course, for every negative Ouija story, there is a positive, uplifting one. The following is an account of what happened to me and three friends recently.

The wheels were set in motion about a month beforehand, when I ran into one of my elderly patients at the supermarket. Jill had been a part of my life since I was a new graduate as her mother, Eve, had been a patient at my clinic for almost twenty years.

"Barbara!" she called out excitedly. "I need you to help me contact Mum in the spirit world! I can't believe I've run into you..."

A little taken aback by her forwardness, I offered my sympathies at Eve's passing. Until that moment, I had no idea that Eve had died. The mother and daughter had been extremely close, having lived together since Jill's short-lived marriage crumbled forty years previously. Seeing Jill without her ever-present sidekick was heart-rending. In all the years I had known them, I had never seen them apart.

"Oh Jill," I said as I put my arms around her. "I'm so sorry..."

Although still smiling, Jill's eyes welled up as she told me that it had been three months since her mother passed away.

"It just isn't getting any easier," she said. "Even though I knew it was coming, it was still such a terrible shock..."

Perhaps I was being a little insensitive, but my initial reaction was to wonder how the death of a 104-year-old could be perceived as shocking. But after a while I reasoned that, of course poor Jill had been blindsided. After all, she and her mother had been each other's sole companions for almost half a century. It would be terrible trying to adjust to life alone.

"Do you think you can help me contact Mum?" asked Jill. "I'm sure she's in the house!"

Within a couple of weeks I had made arrangements to visit Jill with two close friends. We decided to see if we could facilitate contact with Jill and her feisty, elderly mother. So, armed with a Spirit Contact board (which we liked to think only channelled high vibrational, positive energies), we made our way to the old cottage that Jill and her mother had occupied for the last forty years.

I knocked on the door a little after 9.30am whilst my friends, Sherrie and Jacqui, waited in the car. I wanted to make sure that Jill was still keen to try and contact her mother. Although she was visibly nervous, she assured me that this was what she wanted. She needed to make sure that her mother was okay.

Sherrie and Jacqui filed in behind me as we negotiated our way through the nostalgic clutter of four decades. There were statues and dried flower arrangements and an abundance of dust-covered china. Paintings and framed photographs adorned every inch of wall space—a testament to Eve's rich history and a life well-lived.

As we sat at the board, Jill became even more nervous. We joined hands to recite the prayer of protection, and Jill clutched my hand so tightly it felt as though she had no intention of ever letting go. I sensed that her fervour was borne not only from fear, but an intense desire to connect with her beloved mother.

It wasn't long before Eve's buzzing, positive energy began coming through the board, and the planchette began moving towards the letters. Jill gasped as it effortlessly spelled out her mother's name.

Also to put in an appearance were Jill's father, Ned, and her uncle, Percy, both of whom expressed a fierce and protective love for her. They assured Jill that she was extremely loved and protected and told her that they were never far from her side.

Once contact had been established, Jill's spirit family wanted to address a sensitive issue that had been playing on Jill's mind—the matter of Eve's will.

Eve had bequeathed the bulk of her estate equally between her two children: Jill and her elderly brother, Frank. Frank, however, would not have access to his inheritance until his wife, Mary, passed away. This was motivated by the fact that Mary and Eve had had an acrimonious relationship.

But now, in death, Eve had a different perspective. Her and Mary's differences no longer seemed to matter, and she wanted Frank and Mary to have their inheritance now. The planchette whizzed across the board. It seemed Jill's spirit family were desperately trying to make amends for Eve's regrettable decision.

TAKE... MONEY... FRANK, it spelt out.

"You want me to take the money to Frank?" asked Jill.

YES!

Jill rephrased the question time and time again, and each time the spirits assured her that they wanted her to free up the money that Eve had left for Frank.

It seems that in death we gain a fresh and lucid perspective, and hopefully when we do, we are happy with our life's decisions. If, however, we are not, I'd like to think that we can find a way to connect with our loved ones and repair what we feel we didn't do right. It seems that this was certainly one of the main reasons that old Eve was still hanging around the earth plane. Fortunately for her, she not only had a sensitive, receptive daughter, but a team of family members willing to help her from the other side.

In instances such as this, the Ouija board can be a tool which can lead to resolution and good and hopefully help heal the wounds which come from human error. I'm sure that for Jill and her family it was a path to a greater good.

So whilst neither an unwaveringly good thing nor a bad thing, the Ouija board is what the user makes of it. If approached with indifference and a lack of respect, the likelihood of a negative experience increases. If, however, it is used with a loving respect, it can be a tool to help facilitate healing and repair the bonds of love.

As with anything in this world (and quite possibly the spirit world), you reap what you sow. So with regard to my own attitude towards the Ouija board, I will tread cautiously but confidently. I cannot imagine how anything negative can come of what is approached with the highest of respect, positivity and love.

Chapter Nine

The Vengeful Dog

Could this sweet Maltese Terrier be responsible for her vet's near-fatal heart attack?

Although I believe it's possible to use the Ouija board safely, its indiscriminate use can lead to all manner of chaos. Without appropriate preparation and protection in place, the Ouija can channel evil energies which can profoundly impact on the lives of its users. At the very least, it's possible that it may provide a portal for wayward entities who are not necessarily who they say they are.

I believe this may have been the case when some friends of mine spent an evening experimenting with a homemade Ouija board not long after their Maltese Terrier, Becky, passed away. Not imagining for a moment that Becky would come through, the two sisters and their mother were gobsmacked when an entity claiming to be their beloved dog began speaking to them.

"It was really freaky actually," said the girls' mother, Tania. "How can a dog suddenly learn how to spell?"

The freakiest part was the nature of the message itself.

Becky had passed away after her veterinarian, an elderly man named Harold, had miscalculated the dose of Becky's medication, thereby plunging her into an irreversible coma. And now it seemed that Becky was hell bent on revenge, or at least some mischievous entity was trying to make it look that way.

"What was the message?" I asked.

Tania leaned in close amidst the bustle of the busy coffee shop, lest anyone should overhear the bizarre conversation taking place at our table.

"It spelt out *KILL*..." said Tania. "*KILL HAROLD!*"

"No way!" I said, unable to suppress a laugh. Although undoubtedly negative, the thought of a dog exacting revenge on its incompetent veterinarian was so absurd that it was almost comical.

"Hang on, there's more," said Tania's youngest daughter, Ashleigh. "Then it spelt out *HE KILL ME!*"

"Did you feel as though you were really speaking to Becky?" I asked.

"We didn't know what to think," said Tania. "But it really made us feel uneasy."

I wasn't entirely sure what to make of the exchange either. Although I have seen the spirits of animals countless times, I'm not sure whether they would suddenly acquire an ability to spell upon their passing. Also, it was hard to fathom how a sweet little dog could suddenly become angry and vengeful after its death.

Feeling uncertain as to who they were actually speaking with, the three ladies kept up the communication. They kept asking questions, hopeful that there would be some clue as to the real identity of the spirit.

The spirit seemed to be getting more and more agitated, repeating that it wanted to kill Harold. At one point it moved the glass frenetically around the board, repeatedly spelling *KILL, KILL, KILL!*

The glass eventually slowed down, as if it was running out of energy. Then it slowly began to spell out a sentence.

I WANT TO COME HOME.

"By now we were all really emotional, so we decided to end the session. We were completely blown away."

Tania said that the experience unsettled them so much, that she decided to call the veterinary surgery the next day.

"I just wanted to make sure that Harold was okay. Especially since I knew that he was upset about what had happened to Becky..."

"And that's when things got really weird," said Tania, eyes wide as she whispered under her breath. "Harold's receptionist told me that he was in hospital. He'd suffered a massive heart attack the night before!"

Understandably shaken, Tania passed on her best wishes for Harold's speedy recovery and hurriedly got off the phone.

Of course, it could all have just been a simple coincidence, or indeed the stress of causing Becky's death may have precipitated Harold's heart attack. But the fact remains, that someone in spirit was aware of the situation and was suggesting that it was going to make amends.

I put this idea forth to Tania and her daughters, and they agreed that there may indeed have been someone speaking through the board who may have been impersonating Becky.

"Actually, there's been someone in our house for ages," said the eldest daughter, Leah. "There's a dark figure that seems to hang around in the hallway, and sometimes I wake up and feel him in my room."

Leah went on to describe frequent episodes of night terrors, whereby she would wake up in a state of utter panic. These had been tormenting her since her teen years, and were continuing on a regular basis, even though she was now an adult.

She described being woken by a sense of all-consuming terror and was quite often already screaming before she was fully awake. Leah said that she was always drenched in sweat by the time she woke up, and felt as though she had been through a physical ordeal as much as an emotional one. There was always a feeling of heaviness, negativity and oppression in the air; a feeling she found impossible to shake off.

The more details that Leah divulged, the more likely it seemed that the mysterious dark figure could have been trying to impersonate the family dog. It was possible that he'd seized the opportunity to have a joke at the family's expense, hoping to create some drama and distress. Whether he'd actually been involved in Harold's heart attack, however, is debatable. Although I would suggest it's highly unlikely, it's not impossible.

The family went on to recount numerous encounters with the dark entity, many of which were focussed on the sensitive Leah. Now, twenty-six-years-old, she admitted that during her teens, she and a few friends had messed around with a Ouija board and she feels she may have channelled the inky-black ghost that roams the family home. Rare was the night that Leah's bedroom wasn't pervaded by a feeling of intense negativity and heaviness.

"This one particular night when my friends and I were fooling around with the Ouija board, a relative who committed suicide came through. He said that he'd been hanging around our house for a reason. He had something he wanted to tell us," said Leah.

"Did he say what it was?" I asked.

"No," said Leah with a shudder. "I'm not interested in anything he has to say. He was a really nasty man whilst he was alive and I doubt that that's changed. As soon as we realised it was him, we shut the board down."

I asked the family whether the Ouija episode had made any difference to the regular visitations, and they told me that for a little while afterwards, the paranormal activity significantly increased. The ghost seemed ever-more desperate to assert his presence and get his message across.

One late night visitation was particularly terrifying. A sudden cold wind swept into the kitchen, despite all the windows and doors being shut. The chill was accompanied by an overwhelming feeling of dread, and Tania and her daughter, Ashleigh, wasted no time escaping the kitchen's all-encompassing pall of evil.

"Mum and I just stared at each other and then bolted out of there," said Ashleigh. "It absolutely terrified us!"

A week or so prior to our meeting in the coffee shop, Leah had been for a reading with a medium named Fiona. She picked up on the dark entity immediately and confirmed that he was indeed the relative who had committed suicide. It was just as the family had suspected.

Fiona performed a protective ritual to ensure that the ghost's negative influence would no longer affect Leah. She also gave Leah instructions with regard to cleansing the house, stressing how vital it was to clear the family home of the spirit's negativity. The sooner it was done the better.

Fiona told Leah that the ghost wanted to speak to her, but Leah was adamant that the ghost not to be permitted to get through.

"There's absolutely nothing I want to hear from him," she said. "He was a nasty, evil man and I don't want anything to do with him."

She was very firm in her opinion and insisted that Fiona send him away. Respecting Leah's wishes, Fiona put up a protective psychic barrier to shield her from the insistent ghost. She did, however, stress that it was vital that appropriate protective measures were put in place in the family home, to minimize the ghost's impact on those living within its walls.

Leah followed the medium's instructions to a tee, enlisting the help of her mother and younger sister to help cleanse the house. Tania led the threesome in a thorough house-cleansing, wafting the pungent smoke of a smudge stick into each and every room.

"I hope we did it right," said Tania. "We just directed the smoke in every corner whilst telling him to nick off..."

"Is it feeling any different?" I asked.

"Definitely!" she said. Tania went on to tell me that for the first time since the relative's suicide ten years ago, she had managed to enjoy a restful, peaceful sleep. It felt as though a weight had lifted immediately. She also said that as she was performing the cleansing ritual, she was overcome by uncontrollable tear-filled emotion.

"I just couldn't stop crying," she said. "And it seemed like I was more affected in certain rooms. It was as though his energy was concentrated in particular pockets of the house."

Upon reflecting on my coffee date with Tania and her girls, I can't help but wonder whether their nasty relative was being kept earthbound, not only by his own suicide, but by the fact that he had led a self-centred, evil life which had resulted in sorrow and regret.

People who commit suicide usually do so because they can no longer face the pain which plagues their daily lives. In ending their earthly existence, they hope to find oblivion and relief from their suffering. To find themselves still very much aware after death (but without a physical form) would no doubt plunge them into further devastation. More so if they had led less than savoury lives.

What they often don't realise is that healing and unconditional love await them in the light. They prefer to linger in the familiarity of the earth plane rather than venture into the unknown. Indoctrinated belief systems from their earthly lives may have a lot to do with their reluctance to cross over. Many believe that crossing into the light will involve judgement, thereby opening them up to the possibility of being sentenced to an eternity in hell.

In actuality, they are already experiencing their own personal hell, as it is we who judge ourselves. By remaining in the lower astral planes, these souls don't progress and therefore they cannot heal. They are still so connected to the earth that they are acutely aware of the suffering they have caused in life.

Thankfully, this is not true of all suicides, as our spirit guides are quick to intervene, ensuring that the departed soul makes a loving transition to the spirit world. It is only those with complex, unresolved issues who do not readily move on. From what Tania and her girls had told me, it seems that their troubled ghost had too much darkness in his past to allow for an easy transition.

Leah said that after her meeting with Fiona, she wondered whether it might have been better if she had allowed the dark spirit to say his piece. Perhaps he wanted to apologise. It's possible that only then will the family be able to enjoy true peace, once their restless relative's issues are addressed and his soul can finally be at rest.

At this suggestion, Tania said that while she could never forgive her relative for his transgressions, she could possibly find the strength to, at the very least, hear him out. Perhaps giving him the opportunity to express his regret may afford some much-needed peace for both him and his family.

As we parted company that day, Tania left with the intention of contacting Fiona and allowing the troubled soul to come through. It seems that it is the only way that the situation can be resolved.

And as far as the vengeful dog goes, the jury is out for debate. The scenario almost reeks of something conjured up by Hollywood, and I can't help but think it was the dark household energy at play. It's possible that I'm wrong, but I don't think that poor little Becky would have a sinister streak. As her photo attests, she's much too cute! It's more likely that it was an attention-seeking ruse at the hands of a restless spirit—a spirit, who through the loving compassion of his long-suffering family, may finally be put to rest.

Leah, Mike, Tania and Ashleigh pictured at a family celebration in 2013.

Chapter Ten

Lady of the Sea

There is something particularly disturbing about hauntings aboard ships. Imagine being miles out to sea, trapped amongst the restless dead with no means of escape. Perhaps that's why maritime ghost stories have established themselves amongst the scariest of ghostly legends, as their hapless heroes can do little but succumb to the attentions of earthbound spirits.

As well as the classic ghostly legends, there are of course modern day accounts of hauntings at sea. My friend, Adam, experienced his first encounter with a ghost in the middle of the South China Sea, aboard an ex-cruise liner which had been converted into a floating Casino. Adam was employed as the ship's safety officer; a role which included late night security patrols.

Adam pictured during his seafaring days. It seems that Adam's rugged good looks caught the attentions of a restless, female ghost.

Adam could be described as a typical alpha male: well-built, strong, confident and engaging. He isn't prone to flights of fancy, so when he speaks of his close encounter with a distressed female ghost, you just know that his experience is genuine. It was a bewildering experience that affected Adam profoundly and continues to do so to this day. Although it was difficult to process at the time, Adam had no choice but to accept that the ashen woman he encountered at sea ten years ago was a ghost.

Adam's first run-in with the ghost happened at around three-thirty in the morning, whilst he was doing a standard check on the vessel's karaoke rooms. The rooms had been empty and quiet since around midnight, so Adam was taken aback to see a woman walking up the hallway towards him. He reasoned that the white-dressed woman was probably a cleaner, as the ship's cleaning staff wore a white uniform. He called out to her, as the cleaning shift wasn't due to start for at least a couple of hours, and as such she wasn't authorised to be on the deck at this time.

"I thought it was weird that she was ignoring me," said Adam, "as she was definitely close enough to hear me."

The woman simply turned and entered the nearest karaoke room, still not acknowledging Adam's presence.

"I was a bit pissed off by that, so I just followed her in. She was breaching security, and I was all set to tell her off..."

Upon entering the karaoke room, it was soon obvious that there was no one in there. It was as though the woman had simply disappeared. That's when the realisation that he'd just seen a ghost began to sink in.

"I scoured every inch of the room," said Adam, "but she just wasn't there. It was as though she'd vanished into thin air."

Barely able to comprehend what had just happened, Adam left the room as swiftly as possible. There was no explanation other than that the woman he had just been calling out to was a ghost. As the realisation dawned on him, he couldn't help but feel freaked out.

"She looked absolutely solid," he said. "Not at all filmy like I would expect a ghost to be!"

Adam completed the rest of the deck's security checks as quickly as he could and decided to go and broach the subject of the ghost with the Captain.

Unsure how his revelation would be received, he was relieved that the Captain took him seriously and acquiesced to Adam's request to not patrol that deck at night. But it would take more than avoiding Deck 8 to keep the ghost at bay.

A few nights later, Adam was on the verge of drifting off to sleep when he had his second encounter with the ghost. The sense of oppression and claustrophobia are almost palpable as he describes what transpired in his tiny cabin.

"It kind of felt heavy in the room," he said. "There was definitely someone in there with me. It was pitch dark... I couldn't even see my hand in front of my face."

Before Adam could register what was going on, he was assailed by the feeling of someone suddenly throwing themselves on top of him.

"At first I just felt totally paralysed, as though she was sucking up all my energy. It was terrifying, but I also felt extremely mad."

Adam then began grappling with whoever it was on top of him, who by now he was convinced was the woman from the haunted deck.

"And then I said something I feel a bit guilty about now," he said with a grimace. I said, "Get off me you bitch!"

"And did she?" I asked.

"Not straight away, it took some effort to fight her off. And then I was convinced that when I turned on the light, I'd look different somehow. I thought she had drained so much out of me that somehow I'd be skinnier... it was really weird. I felt as though she affected me both physically and emotionally."

As Adam scrambled for the light switch, the woman made her exit. As the comfort of light flooded the small cabin, Adam made his way towards the mirror, fearful of what he might see. But there he was, still his healthy, strapping self, although part of him knew he would never be the same.

Adam was so affected by the encounter that he confided in the wardrobe mistress, a middle-aged Chinese woman who had been working on the ship since its days as a cruise liner.

As he described his first encounter with the ghost on Deck 8 and her subsequent late night visitation, the wardrobe woman's eyes widened. She seemed to know exactly what Adam was talking about.

"You've met Hilary," she said. "She was murdered by her husband outside her cabin... down near what are now the Karaoke rooms. I cleaned up her blood."

Adam was shocked, yet also overcome with compassion. It seemed the woman's ghost had made some kind of connection with him, and what he had perceived to be sinister motives were more likely a cry for help.

Now that he knew who she was, she suddenly didn't seem so scary, and Adam hoped that her poor, distressed soul would be able to find her way into the light.

"Do you think she crossed over?" I asked. "Or did she stay and keep haunting Deck 8?"

Adam wasn't sure if she remained at the scene of her death, because with the Captain's blessing, he no longer patrolled the Karaoke rooms on Deck 8. He didn't want to take the chance of the ghost attaching herself to him again, and following him up to his cabin.

Chapter Eleven

The Unquiet Soldier

As with many people who have an interest in the paranormal, Karen harbours a history of childhood visitations and grew up living in a haunted house.

When I met Karen at a haunting investigation of an old hotel, I was struck by the bravery she displayed when being subjected to the intimidating attentions of a poltergeist. She stoically kept filming with her infrared camera, despite the disturbance steadily escalating in both intensity and violence. Whilst I was reduced to a trembling mess, Karen continued filming with ill-disguised awe. It was as though she couldn't quite believe her luck at capturing the display on camera—a paranormal investigator's dream.

I was further impressed when Karen happily agreed to remain amidst the disturbance alone, whilst I was escorted back to the safety of the public bar area. There was no way that I would have agreed to be alone with the angry poltergeist, and the fact that she did really impressed me.

As we debriefed later that evening, I professed to being utterly impressed.

"Oh, I love all this stuff," she laughed. "I thought that that was awesome!"

"Well, you're much braver than I am," I said and told Karen that I'd lived through five years of poltergeist activity when I was growing up. Re-experiencing the attentions of a poltergeist had stirred up my old memories, effectively turning me into a hyperventilating sook. My heart was still racing even though we'd long since left the haunted corridor where the poltergeist had been metering out his angry display.

Karen told me that she, too, had grown up in a haunted house and that she couldn't categorically say that she never got scared. She admitted that from time to time she still falters, particularly when recalling some of the events that transpired in her childhood home.

The house was built sometime in the 1970s on the site of what was once the Melville army barracks, a twenty minute drive from the city of Perth. Even though she was only four years old at the time, Karen tells me that the house had a bad feeling from the moment they moved in.

Karen's unassuming suburban home in the Perth suburb of Melville.

Karen's older sister was the first to voice her concerns, saying that she thought the house was haunted. Her suspicions about her new home were confirmed not long afterwards, as she soon came face-to-face with its resident ghost. Karen recalls her sister bolting out of her bedroom screaming, insisting that she had just seen a man in green. Of course, when her parents went to investigate, there was no man to be seen, further convincing the terrified young girl that she had just seen a ghost.

The fact that he was wearing army green further fuelled her belief that they were sharing their home with a ghost. It seemed that he didn't realise that the barracks were long gone.

Karen said that there were frequent disturbances, and the feeling of oppression was constant. Lights would go on and off by themselves, and they often heard loud footsteps walking up and down the hall. A negative mood seemed to constantly pervade the home, until ultimately Karen's parents divorced and Karen moved out with her mother and sister.

Her father stayed in the house until his death in 1992, at which time Karen moved back in to look after the place, not without reservation, mind you!

It wasn't long before the familiar feeling of being watched began to assail her, flooding Karen with memories of her childhood experiences in the house. The disturbance quickly escalated to the point where objects would spontaneously fly off the kitchen table and the doors seemed to continually open and shut. Karen's nerves were soon very much on edge.

The more fearful she became, the more palpably the presence manifested, feeding off her emotions as he doled out his daily havoc. Karen could sense that this was not a happy man and was sure that it was the same army ghost who had haunted the house almost thirty years ago. It felt as though the ghost was upping the ante in order to get her to leave.

Things came to a head late one evening as Karen lay on her bed with the bedroom door open. Her room was across the hall from the bathroom, and she could see the towel rail through the open doorway.

Almost imperceptibly, the towel began slowly moving. A moment later it was vigorously whipping back and forth, looking very much as though someone was drying their hands with it. Transfixed by terror and the spectacle of the seemingly possessed towel, Karen remained frozen on her bed, barely able to breathe.

From thereon, the disturbance began to escalate. Taps turned themselves on, gushing water despite the fact that their faucets had been firmly turned off. The frequent sound of footsteps was now not only traversing the hallway, but also making their way into Karen's bedroom. They would stop abruptly at her bedside, causing Karen to run out of the room in terror.

The final straw came late on a Sunday night as Karen was preparing for bed. An insistent banging was coming from the front door, so loudly that it sounded as though the door would burst open at any moment. Seconds later, the noise had transferred to the back door, and from there, to all of the house's windows. Karen peered out nervously, and despite the chorus of insistent banging, there was not a soul to be seen.

Thinking it couldn't possibly get any worse, the banging noises suddenly changed. Now they seemed to be coming from inside the back door. Unable to stand it for another second, Karen grabbed her car keys and bolted out of the front door. She couldn't recall ever feeling so terrified.

After a restless night spent sleeping in her car at the beach, Karen returned to the house with a friend the next day. She packed up all her belongings and moved out, never setting foot in the house again.

Karen is convinced that the streak of light above her is a moving orb — the long-dead soldier further trying to prove his presence.

Karen is convinced that the same ghost that terrorised her family when she was a child was still hanging around the house almost twenty years later. It seems most likely that he was a disgruntled soldier, angered by the fact that strangers had invaded his territory.

The house was subsequently knocked down to make way for a new development, but that may not have been enough to move the uniform-wearing ghost on. Karen tells me that she still drives past from time to time, and whenever she does, she gets that same hollow feeling of dread.

Some experiences leave their indelible mark and can never be entirely erased from one's memory. With those recollections, comes a heavy dose of fear-fuelled nostalgia. So even for someone as brave as Karen, experiences as intense as these are impossible to shake off.

Chapter Twelve

Haunting in Paradise

A haunting needs to get pretty bad for a tough guy like Marcus to move interstate to escape it. Unless you have lived through the experience yourself, it's impossible to fully gauge just how entirely it can consume you. Finding yourself victimised by ghosts invariably undermines your confidence; it infiltrates your life until you can think of little else.

The haunting began in September 2009 shortly after Marcus and his wife, Vickie, moved into their new home. Situated on the Queensland Gold Coast, it looked like any other modern beachside apartment. Its nondescript appearance gave no inkling as to what lay within.

The manifestations began innocuously with the occasional appearance of a fleeting dark figure. Vickie was the first to see the shadowy, black form and presumed that it was Marcus's brother-in-law, Rob. Rob had died as the result of a brain tumour several years earlier, and Marcus often said that he felt him close by. Marcus's brother, Les, had also passed away, although Marcus rarely felt his presence.

Although initially suspecting that the spirit in their apartment was Rob, it soon became obvious that they were not dealing with a benevolent presence. The energy pervading their home was nothing like the positive, loving presence they were used to, and the couple knew that the shadowy figure could not be Rob.

Vickie and Marcus. The couple's relocation to the beautiful Gold Coast turned into a protracted nightmare. © Jane Earle Photography

By the time Marcus went to Sydney two months after moving in, there was an undeniable air of negativity in the household. Despite both being aware of something not being right with their new home, the couple did their best to shrug it off. Even so, Vickie couldn't help feeling uneasy about her husband's impending departure. Marcus was scheduled to have a shoulder reconstruction and would be away from home for two weeks. Having recently started a new job, it wasn't an option for his wife to join him.

As soon as Marcus left, the ghost was quick to pounce upon the chance to exert its bullying behaviour. Having Vickie alone in the apartment would prove to be an opportunity too good to miss. It began on the very first night that Vickie was left alone.

"I was woken by the feeling of someone sitting at the end of my bed," said Vickie. "At first it didn't scare me; it just felt kind of normal. But as I became more aware, I remembered that I was alone in the apartment... and that's when I started to freak out."

Over the course of the fortnight that Marcus was away, the manifestations increased in both their intensity and regularity. There was a constant sense of being watched, and objects began to move around the apartment. Doors and drawers began to open by themselves, and it wasn't unusual for Vickie to come home to find all the kitchen cupboards wide open. It felt as though Vickie was living on the set of a

Hollywood horror movie, never knowing what she would find when she walked through the front door.

She called Marcus in Sydney and told him what was going on; she could no longer keep it to herself. Her husband listened intently, unsure whether to disclose his own frightening secrets.

Realising that Vickie knew that the apartment was haunted anyway, Marcus decided to come clean. He told her that he too had encountered some inexplicable events, but not wanting to scare her, had kept his experiences to himself. As unsettling as it was to feel convinced that their apartment was haunted, it was comforting to know that they weren't alone in their experiences. Whatever lay ahead, they were in this together.

By the time Marcus returned home after his surgery, the couple were seeing the filmy dark figure several times each day. On one occasion it manifested for several seconds, as both Vickie and Marcus watched it come out of the kitchen and walk across the room. It had all become so frighteningly real.

The dark energy began to feel so palpable that they felt constantly under its pall. Not surprisingly, its negativity seemed to intensify in the darkness. So much so, that Marcus and Vickie took to sleeping with the bathroom light on. In some ways this was even worse, as they could then see shadows moving under the door. It felt as though there was no escape.

Sleep was elusive and when it did eventually come, it was often plagued by nightmares. Marcus particularly suffered, and it felt as though the ghost was targeting him with its attentions. Perhaps there was some kudos to be attained by breaking the spirit of such a physically and mentally strong man. It felt as though the ghost was taking perverse pleasure in breaking him down.

Many nights Marcus would be woken by his own screams, and if not by the screams, then by someone persistently poking his arm. He would often find himself mentally awake, but unable to move. In these instances he would summon up every reserve of remaining energy and call out to Vickie. It was as though the entity was sucking out his life force and feeding off his distress. The only way he could get moving would be for Vickie to physically shake his body awake.

Electrical disturbances became commonplace, and the lights would often flick on and off. The fire alarm was repeatedly set off and objects moved of their own accord. Some items would disappear altogether, only to reappear days later in another location (if they resurfaced at all).

A particularly unsettling manifestation was that of a dense, scurrying mass that Marcus and Vickie referred to as the *ghost mouse*. It was a formless, dark blob around the size of a grapefruit that scampered around the apartment like a possessed guinea pig. As comical as it sounds, it radiated negativity and always left a sense of uneasiness in its wake.

It wasn't long before the visual manifestations were accompanied by auditory disturbances, the first of which was an unrelenting banging. The noises were particularly intense at night and seemed to be concentrated at either end of the couple's bed. As if the banging wasn't bad enough, Marcus and Vickie began to hear their clothes hangers being moved around in their wardrobe. It sounded as though somebody was trapped inside it and was clamouring to get out.

It was just a matter of time before the banging was accompanied by voices. Sometimes they just heard giggling coming from the bathroom, and at other times they heard whispering. One voice distinctly addressed Vickie as she sat on the edge of the tub filling her bath.

"Can you hear me?" it said. "We're not going to hurt you..."

Despite the ghost's assurances that it meant no harm, Vickie wasn't convinced. She bolted out of the bathroom as quickly as her trembling legs would carry her. Given its track record, she wasn't convinced of the ghost's harmlessness. Also, the fact that the ghost had said "we" as opposed to "I" unsettled her all the more. Just how many ghosts were they dealing with?

Since the bathroom seemed to be particularly active, Vickie and Marcus decided to leave a video-recorder running overnight, hopeful that they could capture some evidence of the haunting on film. Being proactive gave them some small semblance of control. Perhaps if they reclaimed some power over the situation they wouldn't feel so victimised.

Contrary to what they'd hoped for, accruing solid evidence only made them feel worse. The video footage made their hearts jump into their throats. It showed a bath towel levitate across the full length of the bathroom. To ensure maximum impact, the performance was repeated twice.

As the haunting escalated, so too did the tension within the household. The couple found themselves arguing regularly, to the point where they felt surrounded by constant negativity. The hours of darkness were still the worst, and their nights were disturbed by incessant whispering. It was as though their bed was surrounded by a throng of murmuring ghosts. Before long they decided to vacate their bedroom and moved their bedding into the lounge. It somehow felt less ominous than sleeping in their bed. The light remained permanently on each night.

As a sign of its displeasure, the ghost threw Vickie's favourite clock off the wall, its Betty Boo clock-face shattering in the process.

It got to the point where Vickie and Marcus had no other option than to move out. The ghosts had tormented them for long enough. Fortuitously, a larger apartment in the same complex had recently been vacated, and the couple took it as a sign that it was time to move on. An added bonus was that it was big enough to accommodate Vickie's mother, who was no longer able to live on her own. It seemed as though the new apartment was going to be the perfect solution for them all. The day of the move couldn't come soon enough.

The relocation went smoothly, and by mid-afternoon, everything had been moved to the new apartment. Wanting to ensure that nothing had been left behind, Vickie dashed over to the now empty apartment to do one last walk-through. The sight that greeted her made her even more thankful that they had initiated the move. Every drawer and every cupboard in the entire apartment was open, from the kitchen to the bathroom and the bedroom. It was as if the ghosts were mighty pissed off and eager to display their irritation. Vickie couldn't have felt more relieved that they had finally left. Slamming the door behind her, she bolted to the safety of her new home, little realising that the ghosts were in hot pursuit.

Before long the realisation sunk in—the new apartment was just as haunted as the old one. Human-shaped shadows loitered in the hallways, balls of light dashed across the rooms. Chairs scraped across the floor of their own accord, and a glass bowl was dragged to the edge of the dining table where it perilously teetered and threatened to fall off.

One evening they all watched in muted horror as the long hand of the wall clock rapidly traversed the clock face, spinning around dementedly as if it were possessed.

As the manifestations built up to the level they had been in the old apartment, the stress began to take its toll on Vickie's elderly mother. Within a few weeks of moving in, she was hospitalised with severe chest pains. If anything, the new apartment felt even worse than the old one.

During her mother's stay in hospital, Vickie went into her empty bedroom to discover that the blankets had been pulled down to the end of the bed. The bed had been perfectly made upon her mother's departure, yet now it looked as though someone had just slept in it. She also noticed that her mother's bedside clock had been moved.

Most alarming of all, was the state of the wall print that Vickie had given her mother as a recent gift. It hung off the wall in two distinct halves, having been deliberately ripped straight through its middle.

Vickie removed the print and taped it back together; she didn't want to cause her mother any additional distress. Allowing her to see the damaged print would only alarm her further and quite possibly make her mother feel as though she was being victimised by the ghosts. Vicki returned the damaged picture to its position on the wall, hopeful that her mother wouldn't notice. She needn't have bothered. All hope of the damaged print going unnoticed was quashed within minutes. The print was ripped in half once again, straight through the tape that Vickie had used to repair it.

As in their previous apartment, much of the paranormal activity seemed to be focussed in the bathroom. The smell of aftershave wafted from its recesses, and the toilet brush and flannels were often hurled onto the floor. The drawers were frequently found opened.

As their fear began to escalate, the family began to experience the familiar sounds of banging on the walls, like an irate drumming designed to scare them off.

They also began seeing a dark rod-shaped apparition, the appearance of which often preceded a disturbance. The haunting had reached the point where it had all the hallmarks of poltergeist activity, as more and more physical manifestations began to take place.

Amongst the litany of disturbing events, none was more alarming than when the contents of the family safe went missing. Although always securely locked, when Vickie went to retrieve Marcus's pain medication, every tablet was gone. Also missing were Vickie's mother's diabetes pills and the video recording of the levitating towel in the old apartment. It was all turning into a nasty, psychological game. The ghosts were intent on making them suffer.

At their wits' end, Vickie and Marcus contacted a team of paranormal investigators in the hope of getting to the root of the problem. They wondered if the disgruntled spirits needed help in moving on. Perhaps the haunting was an expression of frustration rather than pure malevolence.

Despite being professional and thorough, the team did little else other than confirm that the apartment was haunted. Contrary to what the couple had hoped for, the manifestations continued as strongly as ever. The team did, however, suggest that all paranormal events were duly documented, and it is from Vickie's meticulous notes that I have been able to accurately reconstruct the details of the haunting. She noted the dates, times and details of every occurrence, going so far as to also record what the weather conditions were like at the time.

As the disturbance continued to escalate, Vickie and Marcus contacted the local Catholic priest and arranged for their home to be blessed. Although the blessing went some way in lulling the activity, the effect was only temporary. The haunting returned to its previous intensity within three days.

Vickie recalls there was one other occasion where there had been a transient lull in paranormal activity. It occurred for no apparent reason, and the threesome were almost too scared to comment on the sudden peace lest they sabotage it. When Marcus finally did see fit to acknowledge the sudden calm, the ghosts took umbrage and amped up their activity yet again.

Marcus's comment of, *I don't think they're here anymore*, was punctuated by a sudden jangling sound, as Vickie's keys and sunglasses spontaneously flew off the bench. They landed in the middle of the floor with a triumphant clatter.

The message was loud and clear—*Oh yes we are!*

It soon became apparent that the ghosts had won, as the family's sense of well-being continued to erode. They were living in a constant state of fear and apprehension and they knew it was time to go.

Despite having expressed their plans to leave, the manifestations continued to gain momentum. It seemed the ghosts wouldn't be satisfied until they were gone.

The trio were assailed by cold bursts of air and the ever-present dark rod-shaped apparition. Pillows were flung from their high shelves and they often heard the furniture moving around in the lounge room at night. The nightly manifestations were accompanied by a sense of being completely paralysed, and Vickie tells me that they would often lie frozen in their beds listening to the ruckus.

Another disconcerting realisation was that the disturbances seemed to be occurring in many of the complex's apartments. Vickie overheard one departing resident say that she just couldn't take it any more; the ghosts were driving her out.

It seems likely that the apartments were built on tainted land. Perhaps it harboured a dark history that no one knew about. Being a relatively new development, it seemed unlikely that anything sinister could have happened in the building itself, and there was no history of deaths within their walls. Of course, there is always the possibility that previous tenants may have dabbled in the occult, thereby opening up a portal to dark energetic realms. Whatever the cause may have been, the fact remained that the building harboured great negativity. Left with no other option, the trio had to get out.

Marcus, Vickie and her mother relocated to Sydney, a good five hundred miles away. The idyllic life they had imagined for themselves in Queensland no longer seemed like a possibility. The haunting had shattered their seaside dream.

Despite the trauma of living through such a harrowing experience, Marcus tells me that there were some positive off-shoots that arose from the drama. For one thing, it gave rise to a desire to help others living through similar situations, and Marcus has since become a highly respected paranormal investigator. Being able to relate to what his clients are going through makes him a compassionate and effective ally when helping those in need.

Even more importantly, Marcus's experiences have awakened a sensitivity which has helped him connect with his brother, Les. Although Marcus was intermittently aware of his brother's presence, his mediumistic gifts have become more honed and have thus afforded clearer spirit communication.

It seems that Les is making use of Marcus's heightened energy and often spells out messages via the family's scrabble board. The scrabble tiles are left permanently out, and Les frequently makes use of them when wanting to say something to his family. The messages are brief (usually just an *I love you* or similar) but enough to send a burst of love and comfort into Marcus's heart.

On one particular occasion, the family were amazed to find a chocolate bar on the scrabble board, next to which Les had spelt out the name *JAKOB*. Jakob is Marcus's son, who wasted no time in gobbling down the gift from his uncle (but not before Marcus had taken a photo of the apported gift)!

Les has also assured Marcus and his family that they will not have to endure the attentions of negative entities again— he will not allow it to happen. Connecting with Les has spiritually empowered Marcus to the point where he cannot imagine being victimised by ghosts ever again; increasing his spiritual sensitivity has given rise to a new level of power.

Whereas fear begets negativity, enlightenment attracts positivity. Marcus and Vickie are surrounded by love and light, and will not allow themselves to be drawn into fear again. So from the most harrowing of times, they have emerged immeasurably stronger and enriched. I dare say the Gold Coast ghosts would be less than impressed!

Chapter Thirteen

Fremantle Ghosts

The harbour city of Fremantle has long been known to be a haven for ghosts. Being the main harbour in Western Australia, it is where the English convicts arrived in the 1800s. Many of these convicts were sentenced to life in the colonies for crimes which were often trivial, no doubt giving rise to considerable human angst. Amongst these harshly sentenced unfortunates were also some genuinely nasty characters, which I expect would readily assume the mantle of angry ghosts.

Fremantle has also been known for housing the state's largest prison, which superseded the original old gaol known as the *Round House*. Both have long since been decommissioned, yet their tortured souls are still believed to roam the prisons' deserted hallways and beyond.

Fremantle's rich and varied history has cemented its reputation for ghosts, which aren't confined to the two old prisons. The Fremantle Arts Centre is considered to be the most haunted building in the Southern Hemisphere, and is certainly not alone with its tales of numerous hauntings. Many Fremantle homes are also believed to be haunted, particularly the old limestone houses which are concentrated around the harbour.

My friend, Vee, spent a year living in one of these old buildings, in a century-old apartment above an army surplus store. She had agreed to house-sit for a friend and began to have doubts about her decision as soon as she walked in the front door.

"There was an awful feeling from the moment you approached the entry," she said. "Even out on the road, which is just up from the Round House."

Vee described the feeling as being overwhelmingly negative and said that it gave her the chills. The feeling pervaded the entry corridor and the stairwell, but seemed to lift once she entered the actual apartment.

"There were ghosts in there too," she said, "but it just didn't feel as heavy. They didn't feel as angry as the ones who were hanging around outside."

When she agreed to house-sit for a friend, Vee (pictured with husband, Leo) did not expect to be roommates with a ghost.

Her initial thought was to retract her offer to house-sit, but reasoned that since she felt okay inside the house (and was particularly at ease in the main living area) she would bite the bullet and stay.

"You've got ghosts, you know," she said to her friend, Paul.

"Really?" he asked with a bemused smile. It was obvious that he wasn't convinced.

As soon as she was alone in the house, Vee began to tune in to the apartment's ghosts. At first it was just an intense feeling of an unseen presence and seemed to be focussed around the main bedroom. Although she didn't feel unduly threatened, Vee took to sleeping in the family room. She told the ghosts that they were welcome to stay, under the condition that they didn't actually show themselves. Vee knew that if she saw one of the apartment's ghostly residents she would find it difficult to stay there. As brave as she was sharing the apartment with ghosts, she knew that her bravado would come crashing down around her if she saw one face-to-face.

"So I just slept on the sofa, as that's where I felt safest," said Vee. "Even though one of them followed me in there and woke me up!"

Vee said that she was dozing on the sofa, when she was woken by an amazingly beautiful smell. She said it was overwhelming, yet lovely, smelling very much like freshly picked peaches. It seemed to have just wafted out of nowhere.

"My first thought was that it was an angel," said Vee. "Or at the very least a really beautiful spirit."

She said that the sweet-smelling spirit was not the only presence in the home, and despite requesting that the ghosts not show themselves, one of them saw fit to appear to Vee on the stairwell.

"Well, I saw his reflection actually," said Vee. "I was coming down the stairs and I saw him in the mirror."

Vee described the ghostly gentleman in vivid detail, and it sounded as though he may have been an old sea captain. He had a bushy, grey beard and wore a peaked naval cap. A pipe hung from his mouth.

Vee said that she absolutely freaked, especially since the ghost looked deceptively solid. It was as though an old man had stumbled into her home from a bygone era.

Too terrified to do anything else, Vee stood frozen on the staircase. She was, however, too scared to look at the apparition, so she turned her back to the mirror until she was able to compose herself and continue on her way. Recounting the experience now, Vee is quick to laugh at herself. She assures me that at the time, it was certainly no laughing matter.

And as much as the old captain had scared her, Vee said that the scariest thing about the apartment was Paul's choice of paintings. Paul was particularly proud of his collection of Venetian clown paintings, which unfailingly gave Vee the chills. The clown faces looked sinister and foreboding, and were creepy enough to set off a clown phobia in the sanest of individuals! Vee couldn't stand them and asked Paul if he minded if she moved them out of sight for the duration of her stay.

Since these were expensive treasures and Paul's pride and joy, he refused to remove the paintings from the wall, even during his absence.

Interestingly, his most expensive piece was an original artwork procured from the Queen Mary. Vee found this painting similarly disturbing, although the clown faces were by far the worst. I did wonder whether the painting had any connection to the old sea captain, and couldn't help but think he may have been keeping a watchful eye on part of his ship's treasures.

At any rate, the clowns stayed stubbornly hanging from their hooks, tormenting Vee whenever she walked past. Until, that is, someone decided to intervene.

Vee was shocked to awaken one morning to find the clown painting she hated the most had been flipped over so that it was facing the wall. No one else had been in the apartment for days.

Although Vee was definitely unsettled by the episode, she couldn't help but feel slightly amused. She wondered if the sea captain had taken a shine to her and was possibly trying to please her by hiding the offending picture.

Paul, of course, wasn't as amused upon his return home and naturally thought that Vee had turned his painting over.

"And you know what?" said Vee. "I didn't even tell him that it wasn't me who did it. He'd think I was a fruit loop if I told him it had been done by a ghost!"

As unsettling as it sometimes felt knowing that her room mates were ghosts, Vee came away with fond memories.

Although they had undoubtedly scared her, she knew that she was never in any peril.

"After all, how bad could they be if they hated the paintings too? It seems as though we had something in common!"

Or, at the very least, they were trying to please her. Vee agrees and smiles at the memory, wondering how she could ever have imagined the apartment's ghosts to be anything but benign. The clowns though, are another matter altogether!

Chapter Fourteen

Late Night Visitors

Spirits are able to manifest wherever they please, but perhaps we are just more sensitive to their energy in quiet, dark rooms. That said, if the energy is powerful enough, spirits can command our attention in the most unlikely of situations or environments.

My father will vouch for this, as he experienced one of his most striking spirit encounters in the middle of a bustling airport as he sat waiting for his flight home from New Caledonia.

One moment he was quietly reading whilst intermittently sipping his drink and the next he was watching his glass move by itself across the table. And in what was to be the grand finale, the glass simply exploded, splattering its entire contents of red wine.

The woman sitting four feet away on the other side of the table immediately became defensive.

"I didn't touch it!" she said. "I was nowhere near it!"

My father assured the woman that he knew she hadn't touched the glass. She obviously hadn't seen the glass sliding across the table beforehand or else she would have realised that something supernatural was at play.

My father had frequent inexplicable experiences during his time working as an engineer in New Caledonia, and they were often deeply disturbing. He suspects that the negativity he encountered there may have been connected with New Caledonia's somewhat 'unsavoury' past. Cannibalism was rife in the region up until the nineteenth century, and some believe it is haunted by the tortured souls of the cannibalised. Perhaps the souls of the cannibals themselves have struggled to find peace and continue to roam the place where they committed their disturbing acts.

Regardless of history, however, it must be said that spirits and ghosts can pretty much turn up anywhere. All types of people from all walks of life have been privy to the wonders of the spirit world, and the nature of their experiences varies as widely as they do.

One thing, however, is consistent with them all. A taste of the paranormal usually profoundly affects those who experience it. And as frightening as these encounters can sometimes be, they offer a precious and irreplaceable gift.

They bring with them the conviction that life goes on despite physical death. With that comes the comforting assurance that love never dies. Our loved ones remain connected to us irrespective of what happens to the body which contained them. The fate of our physical shell is irrelevant; it's the survival of the soul which bears the most meaning. Our spirit-selves never die, the essence which makes us 'us' is eternal.

So although spirits can (and indeed do) turn up just about anywhere, to my mind the most frightening apparitions are those which take you by surprise in your bedroom. At least in situations where you have willingly placed yourself amongst ghosts (such as when investigating haunted locations), you have time to mentally prepare for your paranormal encounter. But when an apparition presents itself without the slightest warning, the shock factor escalates and makes the encounter so much more frightening. These late night, surprise drop-ins are much more frequent than we would dare imagine.

It's long been known that the human mind is most receptive in the sleep state, hence the accurate dream messages which often filter through. Many people also report dream visitations from deceased family members—interactions that are so vivid that the dreamer is convinced they have actually spent time with that person. And rather than waking and feeling disappointed that their dream isn't real, they often awake with an overwhelming sense of joyousness, convinced that they have just spent time with their loved one in another dimension. When people tell me about their dream interactions, I generally ask them how they felt upon awakening. The euphoric feeling of being reunited with someone they thought they would never see again is the dead giveaway. It's as though the visitation with their loved one has somehow touched their soul, and deep inside they just know that the encounter was real.

Less subtle visitations involve spirits manifesting vividly enough to be seen in the waking state. Rather than just appearing on the astral plane and interacting through dreams, these spirits actually appear in the earth plane and may exert an effect on the physical environment.

I have spoken to countless people who have woken abruptly to find a figure looming over them, most often beside them or at the end of the bed. These are described as anything from pale luminescent figures to solid lifelike apparitions or disturbingly, dark shadow people. Again, because the mind is only just out of the sleep state, it is receptive enough to observe spirit energy. Although these same figures could present themselves in the middle of the day, they would be less likely to be seen as a result of the overload of sensory stimulus which we contend with when we are fully awake.

Upon discussing the subject with a friend, she described an encounter which affected her profoundly. Although she found the experience terrifying, I'm not convinced that Rachel's visitation was as sinister as it first seemed.

Rachel was woken by a sense of presence in her bedroom and she was convinced that someone had just come in. She opened her eyes cautiously, almost too frightened to look into the darkness.

When she did, she couldn't help but gasp. A filmy mass was floating around the bedroom, heading towards her husband's side of the bed. A moment later it was floating above him, and then in one swift movement, it disappeared straight into her husband's body. His body jerked abruptly, but despite this, her husband continued his deep, untroubled sleep.

Rachel was absolutely terrified and lay frozen on the bed. It seemed as though an entity had just taken over her husband's body, and the thought of it made her feel sick.

"And then it got even more full on," said Rachel. "From out of the darkness, someone suddenly grabbed my arm. The worst part was that it was so dark that I couldn't see a thing!"

I imagined that by now, Rachel would have been feeling even more terrified, but surprisingly, she said she was not. If anything, whoever it was holding her arm was making her feel much better. It was as if somebody was trying to comfort her.

"It kind of felt like a good grab," said Rachel. She later told me that she suspected that it may have been her brother in spirit, as it definitely felt comforting.

"I still woke my husband up though; it was hard to just forget about it and go to sleep!"

Being somewhat of a sceptic, her husband took in the details of the supposed visitation with a grain of salt. Rachel, however, was convinced that she had experienced a spirit visitation, and despite her initial fear, she felt privileged to have seen what she did. She also couldn't help wondering if the vision connected to her husband had something to do with the fact that he had been ill for the best part of a year. She asked me what I thought.

In my experience, quite often things we perceive to be confronting or negative are in actuality positive interactions.

I told Rachel that I felt that the white mist that had entered her husband's body was more than likely to be his etheric form. When we sleep, our astral bodies are free to detach from us and travel through higher vibrational dimensions. They do, however, remain connected via an etheric silver cord, which guides us back to our bodies once our astral travelling is done.

The fact that Rachel had been so fearful at seeing the mist, had then probably lead to the manifestation of

Rachel's arm grabbing spirit guide. It seems that he was trying to reassure her that all was fine.

Since there have been no further manifestations since this episode, and certainly no negative repercussions related to the body-invading mist, it seems that this is likely to be the most probable explanation for Rachel's late night visit.

Not all visitations are so benevolent, and many have the capacity to leave their experiencers utterly terrified.

Returning to my father's experiences in New Caledonia, a late night bedroom visitation had a much greater impact than his airport encounter. It is an experience that he will never forget.

My parents, Luka and Marica, pictured in 2014. My father's enthusiasm at being appointed chief engineer in New Caledonia was thwarted by the attentions of a malevolent spirit.

My father was woken up by the sense of someone being in his room, which was one of many small transportable buildings dotted around the camp. He felt as though they were rummaging around in his belongings, and his first thought was that someone had broken in to steal something.

The sense of presence was unmistakeable, so he went to reach for the lamp switch. Before he could do so, however, he was assaulted by a sudden, unremitting weight on his chest, with which he then began to grapple.

He and the unseen entity were soon engaged in both a physical and mental battle, as my father thrashed around the room trying to break free. Throughout the encounter, the entity was either pressing on his chest or clinging to his back. My father cursed and demanded that it should leave. His adrenaline was keeping him fighting, but he felt utterly terrified. He'd never experienced anything like it.

After what felt like hours, but was probably no more than a couple of minutes, the weight disappeared as swiftly as it had first appeared. The room still felt oppressive and frightening, as though the entity had left a pall of negativity in its wake.

My father said that it was the first time in his life that he had been truly frightened, and the experience affected him for weeks. Although a well-balanced and strong man, he had been utterly intimidated by the unseen presence. He refused to sleep with the light off until he returned home to Perth a week later, hopeful that the light would deter whatever negativity was lurking around the camp.

Encounters such as my father's are frequently documented, however, not all are due to a paranormal visitation. Thankfully, in many instances, the experience has a physiological aetiology, unlike my father's encounter which involved an actual entity.

Old Hag Syndrome (a terrifying term in its own right!) is the phrase coined to describe debilitating cases of sleep paralysis, whereby the body is still asleep, but the consciousness has roused to the point where the mind is awake. The fact that the body is still physically asleep, gives the impression that one has been paralysed and is quite often accompanied by a feeling of pressure on the chest.

In order to differentiate between genuine paranormal assault and an attack by the fictitious old hag, one needs to assess the sequence of events which occurred and assess all the facets of the visitation. I dare say that in most instances, the experience will be nothing more than an episode of sleep paralysis. But when it is not, it can be the most terrifying experience of one's life.

Less sinister night visits are where spirit guides or deceased loved ones proceed to seat themselves on your bed. This is something that I experience often and is usually accompanied by a gentle buzzing sensation coursing through my mattress. Despite having these experiences for several years, and knowing that they are harmless, these visits are still able to unsettle me and culminate with me turning on my bedside lamp! I also often feel my hair or my leg being stroked, as though someone is trying to soothe me.

A young friend is going through this very experience as I write, and her night time visitor returns night after night. She has taken to sleeping with the hallway light on and sleeps with her giant teddy bear so that there is less room on the bed for a ghost! Although I have assured her that the presence means her no harm, my soothing reassurances are somewhat hypocritical. As even after all these years of experiencing ghostly visitations myself, I'm still a little anxious during this type of encounter. I imagine that's because it is so palpable; there is no mistaking the weight on the bed or the gentle touch of a human hand. It's thrilling and frightening all at once.

The fact remains that the most likely place that you will see a spirit is late at night in your bedroom. You can go on all manner of ghost hunts and spend hours exploring haunted locations, but the truth is that spirits are around us no matter where we are.

The comforting thought is, that more often than not, our late night visitors are most likely to be our departed friends and family, and of course, our spirit guides. So if you waken to the sight of a ghostly visitor, try to be braver than me and not allow yourself to be scared. Embrace it for what it is—

reassurance from the other side that the human spirit lives on. More often than not, the ghostly apparition lingering in your bedroom is someone that you love very much, just checking in to say *hi*!

Chapter Fifteen

Stay Behinds... the unseen house guests

To the sensitives among us, some homes positively scream of the ghosts which linger within their walls. I remember the moment I first walked into our soon-to-be family home when I was seven years old. It was the mustiness that struck me first—the dank smell which comes from being closed up and uninhabited for too long. The carpets caught my attention as well, ugly and stained, they reeked of damp. But beyond the assault on my physical senses, there was something which was much less obvious. Despite its relative subtlety, it was, however, just as offensive. An inexplicable heaviness struck me to the middle of my core, an oppression that seemed to hit me in my solar plexus. It's a feeling that I associate now with the presence of ghosts.

Back then, I discovered the presence of our unseen housemates the hard way, with a steadily increasing display of paranormal activity. It continued to escalate until there was no denying that we were sharing our house with ghosts, and even then, it took some persuasion until we eventually moved out.

In most instances, negatively motivated hauntings are a battle to mark one's territory. The ghost is often someone who once lived in the house and considers the new occupants to be intruders. Sometimes the ghosts are happy to live side-by-side with the new residents, but in more hostile cases, they are hell-bent on getting the current occupants out.

Thankfully, most hauntings are fairly benign, many of which are little more than psychic replays of long-gone events. Of the intelligent hauntings, or hauntings which involve an actual sentient spirit, a small proportion may indeed be quite aggressive. On the other end of the spectrum, most ghosts are happy to dwell side-by-side with the living residents, rarely manifesting in more than subtle, unobtrusive ways.

Ever since my first book was published in 2012, I have been approached by numerous people wanting to share their own haunted histories. It has made me realise that hauntings and paranormal phenomena are not as rare as I once thought.

Joan is an old school friend, whose childhood home wasn't far from my own. Joan's family moved into their 1950s house when she was fifteen. Since it wasn't quite big enough to accommodate the whole family, Joan's father enclosed the back veranda which served as Joan's makeshift bedroom.

Joan experienced her first visitation on the very first night spent in her new bedroom.

"I was woken by three loud knocks," she said. "They were coming from underneath the concrete floor, and I just couldn't understand how that could be possible."

Joan tried to work out the source of the unmistakeable rapping, thinking there must have been a logical explanation. Before she had time to come to any sort of conclusion, the source of the three knocks materialised right before her eyes.

Joan watched in terrified awe as a young girl (probably of a similar age to herself) appeared in front of her wardrobe. The girl was sitting cross-legged on the floor and was visible for several seconds.

Joan was frozen with fear and lay transfixed by the vision before her. Once the girl disappeared, she was able to get up and bolt from her room.

From then on, Joan experienced frequent visitations. It seemed the girl could relate to her and was therefore drawn to her more than anyone else in the house. She would often turn on Joan's stereo and music would play loudly in her room. It made no difference whether the stereo was plugged in or not, the music would play regardless.

Joan also reported that the visits were often preceded by the knocking which makes me wonder whether the young girl was politely announcing her arrival.

Although the ghostly girl was by no means sinister, the teenage Joan couldn't help feeling frightened by her attentions. She took to sleeping with a night light, a habit that she cannot break to this day.

Joan seems to have an affinity for ghostly attention as her experience with the teenage girl was not her first encounter with spirits. Prior to moving into the 1950s house, she lived a few miles away in a suburb called Cannington. It was here that Joan had her first contact with ghosts.

She was only eight years old when they first moved into the house in Cannington, and again, it didn't take long for its ghostly inhabitant to appear to her. Joan was in her bedroom when she heard a noise coming from the window, and she looked up to see the face of a distraught-looking man.

"I can still picture him to this day," said Joan. "He was wearing a checked, flannel shirt and he had straggly, blonde hair."

Joan screamed for her father, who burst into the room within seconds. By then, the man had disappeared, which prompted Joan's father to go chasing after him outside.

"And of course there was no sign of him," said Joan. "No footprints, nothing!"

The man continued to put in infrequent appearances, and seemed to gravitate towards Joan. It didn't take long before it sunk in that the man was actually a ghost, a realisation that terrified young Joan all the more.

The family were to later discover that an electrician had fallen off the roof of their home a couple of years before they moved in. He died at the scene as a result of his injuries, prompting the family to believe that the check-shirted ghost was indeed the hapless electrician, especially since he always seemed to be loitering outside, seemingly haunting the scene of his untimely death.

Not all spirits who linger on the earth plane are confused or unhappy, some stay behind for benevolent reasons. This was the case with a lady named Kristen's father-in-law. Kristen told me that she always suspected that her father-in-law was around, but it took a near fatal-incident to confirm that Kristen's suspicions were true.

Following the death of her husband, Kristen's mother-in-law came to live with Kristen's family in a self-contained granny flat. Although connected to the house, the granny flat had an independent telephone line so that the elderly woman could call upon her son and daughter-in-law should she need any help.

Late one evening as Kristen and her son sat watching television, the telephone rang—the caller ID identifying the call as coming from the granny flat at the other end of the house. Upon answering, the only sound to be heard was that of the television.

Kristen instantly thought that her mother-in-law was in trouble and worried that she had perhaps had another fall. Not wasting a moment, Kristen and her son dashed to the granny flat only to find that its small kitchen had become engulfed in thick smoke. The kitchen bench was smouldering as the fire began to take hold. Meanwhile, Kristen's mother-in-law was fast asleep in her bedroom. With her door shut, she was oblivious to the fire starting in her kitchen. The telephone, which sat on her bedside, was still firmly on the hook.

A heavy smoker, the woman had emptied her overflowing ashtray into the kitchen bin before bed, little realising that her final cigarette was not fully extinguished. Within minutes a fire had started up in the bin, and was now starting to spread throughout the kitchen.

Kristen and her son quickly extinguished the growing flames, averting disaster with minutes to spare.

Upon reflection, Kristen is convinced that her father-in-law was responsible for the mysterious phone call.

"I really think my father-in-law saved us," she said. "If it wasn't for that phone call, the entire house could have burned down..."

Food for thought, indeed.

The most disturbing stay behinds are those who will stop at nothing to drive out their home's new occupants, going to great lengths to ensure their bullying tactics reap the results that they're after. Their ghostly manifestations are a nasty campaign of relentless intimidation, often increasing in intensity until they achieve their desired outcome.

My friend, Mark, is a fellow podiatrist, and we have been friends since I was a new graduate working in private practice. Mark is a level-headed professional, yet when his elderly patient, Bob, told him about the frequent disturbances in his home, he just had to sit up and take notice. Bob was reaching out to him for help; he was unsure who else he could talk to.

The elderly gent was becoming increasingly disturbed by a pair of nasty entities in his rental home. It was obvious that they were not at all happy about Bob being there and were doing their best to frighten him off. It began fairly insidiously with strange noises and banging, but had now escalated to actual voices calling out and abusing him.

The ghosts were also often moving Bob's belongings and hiding them, behaviour which was causing him no end of frustration. They also took to making *one hell of a racket*, as he described it, particularly when he was trying to go to sleep. In desperation, Bob set up a voice recorder prior to going to bed. He wanted to validate what he was experiencing and be able to listen to the recordings to try and work out what it was the ghosts wanted. One of the pair was particularly aggressive, and his guttural, nasty taunts can be heard on the tape.

There was no denying that the old widower was sharing his home with ghosts.

Mark suggested that perhaps I could help resolve Bob's troublesome situation, and I was more than happy to help.

Although I have called Bob to arrange a time to meet up, I have yet to visit his home and investigate the haunting. I suspect, however, that when I do, I will come up against some disgruntled, unhappy entities, as opposed to anything truly malicious. In the majority of cases such as these, the disturbed spirits are displaced souls trying to assert their authority. They are merely standing their ground in what they imagine to still be their home. In many instances, ghosts such as these haven't fully grasped that they are dead, and can't understand why strangers have invaded their territory. I feel confident that with a compassionate approach and some persistently gentle persuasion, I will be able to calm the disturbance and help the ghosts move on.

If my suspicions are not correct, however, and poor Bob is up against some genuinely nasty entities, I will waste no time in calling for back up. I'll let you know how I go.

Chapter Sixteen

The Mischief Makers

For every positive story about spirit contact, there is invariably a slightly more sinister one. This particular ghost story belongs to the latter group, whereby indiscriminate dabbling led to some less than savoury ghostly goings on.

For those who carelessly open the doors to spirit communication, it is important to be aware that negative energies are just as likely to come through as positive ones. This is particularly true if appropriate protection is not in place.

Certain modalities of communication, most pointedly the Ouija board, are more likely to channel earthbound ghosts as opposed to higher vibrational, crossed-over energies. As such, there are likely to be negative or unhappy emotions to contend with, or problems to be resolved. Ghosts have not crossed over for a reason, and that reason usually becomes apparent throughout the course of the communication.

There are generally four reasons why a soul doesn't progress to the higher realms of the spirit world after death. The first, and probably most common reason, is that they do not immediately grasp the fact that they are dead. Consequently, they remain trying to go about their daily business on the earth plane. By the time they comprehend that they no longer have a physical body, they are quite often disorientated and unsure as to how to progress. This is particularly true for those whose death is unexpectedly abrupt; it takes a while for the realisation that they are dead to sink in.

The second most likely explanation as to why a soul doesn't cross over is largely borne out of fear. Some souls consciously choose to remain on the earth plane because it feels familiar and safe. Going towards the light represents venturing into the unknown, and many souls find this concept terrifying. As such, they resist moving towards it, preferring to remain in a twilight state between the living and the dead. It is not a particularly fulfilling existence, and as such theses souls are rarely, if ever, happy.

Another reason why the dead remain earthbound is that they have led less than savoury lives whilst living. Their refusal to cross over is often borne out of fear of judgement, and by avoiding crossing over, they feel they are escaping punishment for their bad deeds. What they fail to grasp is that when we become spirits, it is we who judge ourselves. We learn from our transgressions and hopefully grow from our experiences, whether they are positive or negative. By not evaluating the lives they have just left, these souls relinquish the opportunity to grow from their mistakes. In effect, they are punishing themselves by remaining earthbound. Needless to say, these souls are quite often enshrouded in negativity, and their poor choices in life continue to enslave them.

Last of all, some choose not to cross over because they feel there is unfinished business to be attended to on the earth plane. This can be noble in nature (for example, a desire to keep an eye on one's children) or is perhaps motivated by less-honourable intentions such as revenge.

The crux of the matter is that earthbound energies are not fulfilling their spiritual potential, and as such are unlikely to be happy. Consequently, channelling these ghosts opens one up to the possibility of negative experiences, and those who open the doors to the lower vibrational realms need to be mindful of this.

The owner of a local grocery store is well aware that this is true. What began as a little harmless dabbling to fill in the time became a tiresome headache when the ghosts she attracted refused to go away.

"We used to just grab some cardboard and rustle up a Ouija board when we were bored," Lily told me. "Then the staff and I would huddle at the back of the shop and ask if any spirits wanted to come through."

"And did they?" I asked.

"Absolutely!" said Lily.

Since Lily's store was situated in the middle of a busy shopping centre, it was surrounded by the constant buzz of activity. The energy generated by large groups of people is very attractive to ghosts, as they use the energy of the masses to sustain them. They are drawn to activity and crowds.

At first, the ghosts who came through were relatively harmless, but as time went on, their behaviour became more disagreeable. One ghost claimed to be a little boy, and at first he interacted as one would expect of a young child. With subsequent visits, however, he became increasingly nasty. His language deteriorated, and he called Lily and her staff the vilest names he could think of.

"In the end I doubted whether he was a child at all," said Lily. "Ghosts aren't necessarily who they say they are... some of them like to play games."

Over the course of a few weeks, the ghost boy and his cohorts began to get progressively more domineering. They would demand that the windows were closed during their séances, whereas Lily preferred to leave them open.

"It felt as though they were trying to concentrate their energy," she said. "We just refused point blank, as we were worried they were trying to create some kind of portal. They were starting to creep us out."

Lily said that the ghosts seemed to be trying to intimidate them, and on one occasion they even blew out their candle. It had turned into a power play, and Lily refused to succumb to being scared. She knew full well that that was exactly what the ghosts wanted.

The supposed boy ghost went from being a sweet and unassuming presence to someone with ill-disguised malevolence. Worst of all, it was getting harder and harder to end each séance as the ghosts were refusing to step back. If a ghost doesn't move to the word *GOODBYE* on the Ouija board, it means that their energy is still present. As such, it can continue to feed off the energy of the participants and may well have a negative effect on their lives.

It wasn't long before the other store owners got wind of what had been happening at the back of the grocery store. They were less than impressed and were worried that Lily and her staff's dabbling could draw negativity into their stores too. The coffee shop owner was particularly irate.

"He came bustling over one morning in a right state," said Lily. "He said that things had been flying off the top of his fridge. He was convinced that it had something to do with us."

And indeed, an inexplicable heaviness seemed to have pervaded the surrounding stores, and Lily agreed that it may have had something to do with the ghosts they had attracted with their spur of the moment séances.

"Getting them to leave was the hard part," she said, "especially when it came to trying to end a session. We discovered that they didn't like discussing the light, and mentioning God was also a no-no. As soon as God came up in the conversation, they'd immediately withdraw. So in the end, we used that as our trick, as any mention of God or crossing over had the planchette scurrying across to *GOODBYE*."

"And I always like to burn my Ouija boards," said Lily. "That's why I only ever use homemade ones. You just never know what sort of negative energy is left lingering within the board... as far as I'm concerned, it's best to get rid of it!"

I asked her if she had been put off from using the Ouija after this period, especially since she had encountered such blatant negativity. I won't repeat exactly what the supposed boy ghost called her, but needless to say, it was one of the most derogatory terms you could think of. His contempt for Lily and her staff was obvious. Didn't she worry that he would attach to her and bring his negativity into her home?

"Not at all," she said. "They're just mischief makers. I knew that they couldn't hurt us."

Lily went on to tell me that as far as she was concerned, keeping the upper hand was the key. Believing in one's own strength was paramount.

"After all," she said, "What can they do to us? We're the ones with the bodies!"

She also believes that keeping a handle on one's fears is vital.

"If they know that you're scared, you're in big trouble," she said. "They latch onto you and feed off your fears... it makes them feel as though they have the upper hand."

Fortunately for Lily, she has always had a strong disposition, so her irresistible attraction to the paranormal hasn't landed her in strife. For the rest of us, however, we need to be mindful of the pitfalls of dabbling in the unknown, particularly in ways which may attract opportunistic energies. Whilst a ghost can't physically harm you, they can severely affect your sense of well-being. Having lived through a five-year haunting myself, I can assure you that this is most certainly true.

My advice is to tread carefully, especially if you are experimenting within a group of similarly inexperienced people. Opening doors to other realms can be fraught with danger, and unless it is done carefully, can lead to all manner of disturbances. If you are drawn to such pursuits, only approach once you are armed with an armoury of knowledge and barrage of protection. If you have any doubts about what you are doing, then don't approach at all. It's better to forfeit the experience of a séance, than to get more than you bargained for. As once the doors to the spirit world have been opened, they can prove difficult to close.

Chapter Seventeen

Uncle Eugene

There are two strong beliefs that I have with regard to the paranormal. First of all, those who have died continue to watch over their loved ones, either as subtle, benevolent presences, or as more obvious, insistent ones. I also believe that significant trauma (whether it be emotional or physical) can increase our sensitivity to the spirit energies around us. This is never more true than in the case of near death experiences. It's thought that once we have teetered at the interface between life and death, we become more in tune to the spirit world. If we are given a glimpse of otherworldly realms, it changes us forever. We can't undo that which we have experienced, or 'un-see' what we have seen. Sometimes those experiences which begin as the most painful and harrowing end up being the ones which most enrich us. It is from the most difficult of circumstances that we ultimately grow. This certainly seems to be the case with regard to my neighbour, Richard.

I was sitting on my back deck enjoying a late spring afternoon when Richard sauntered over to retrieve his young son. The children had been playing in the backyard, and I had been keeping an eye on them from the deck. I was contemplating writing the next chapter of my book, but hadn't quite made up my mind as to what I was going to write about.

Little did I know that my neighbour was going to decide for me, as what he was about to tell me soon had me rushing to the keyboard. Sometimes the most inspiring stories assail us when we least expect it, and with regards to Richard's recollections of his Uncle Eugene's passing, this was certainly one such case.

Eugene, who lived in Ireland, was in his early forties when he was fatally electrocuted. His family and friends were, of course, devastated as he had been a much loved and vibrant addition to their lives. His sudden passing had left a gaping, painful hole. In his early twenties, Richard felt his loss profoundly as he had always felt a strong connection to his uncle. To make matters worse, he was living on the other side of the world in Australia and felt helpless as his aunt and cousins struggled through their loss in Ireland.

Further drama was just around the corner as Richard almost found himself following the same path as his uncle just a month after his death. Richard was crossing the road when he was run over by an inattentive driver; his ragdoll body was flung up and over the car's windscreen. It was astonishing that he wasn't killed, as the driver was hurtling towards him at considerable speed. Although he physically recovered without any permanent injuries, he was, however, forever changed. The experience had given rise to an innate sensitivity he did not previously possess, as his psychic abilities seemed to spring forth as a result of his accident.

Richard's increased sensitivity began manifesting innocently enough as he started to experience episodes of precognition. He was given glimpses of future events moments before they occurred, which was particularly handy when anticipating the location of speed cameras!

His sensitivity escalated to the next level when his Uncle Eugene visited him in a dream. Disturbingly, he showed himself as a skeleton. When the departed show themselves in an unsettling physical state, it generally indicates that their soul is still earthbound. In Eugene's case, there were two likely reasons for his reluctance to move on.

First and foremost, his death had been sudden and untimely. Accidental deaths often leave the deceased disorientated, and they can therefore still have a strong attachment to the earth plane. These souls cannot always fully grasp that they've died, and as such they remain in the environment which feels safe and familiar. Even when the realisation that they're dead eventually does sink in, there is still a reluctance to cross into the light. They are often concerned about the impact of their death on their family and may be tethered by a sense of obligation or a desire to complete unfinished tasks.

In relation to Eugene, it seems that both of these were true. He was worried about the welfare of his wife and children and was particularly disturbed by the fact that he had left the household in utter chaos. Eugene had been midway through a renovation when he was killed, leaving a half-done bathroom amongst a household of disarray. He couldn't rest easily until the job was completed. He asked Richard if he would help.

Richard had no choice but to agree to his uncle's wishes; ignoring his uncle's plea was not an option. To the ill-disguised astonishment of his family, Richard announced that he was moving to Ireland. He was to stay with his aunt and cousins for the next nine months.

Upon his arrival, his aunt announced that she knew he would be coming all along. It seems that she too was privy to some otherworldly information. She was informed by a clairvoyant that Eugene would be sending help in the form of his nephew from Australia.

Richard plodded away at the renovation month after month, happy in the knowledge that his uncle would be gleaning comfort and peace from his efforts. There was no greater sense of achievement than when the job was finally done.

After he'd finished, Richard rewarded himself with a trip around Ireland. He felt as though he was finally able to leave Eugene's family, safe in the knowledge that he had done his uncle's bidding. He did not expect to be called upon again, but that's exactly what happened on Christmas Day. Despite being on the other side of Ireland, Richard was overcome by the need to drive back to his aunt's house. The nagging feeling that she needed him just wouldn't go away.

He jumped into his car and made the trek across the country, arriving sometime in the early evening. He found his aunt sitting in the kitchen looking lonely and miserable, a half-burnt cigarette in her hand. She had settled in for a Christmas night alone, as Richard's cousins had all gone away. His aunt had not wanted him to know that she was spending Christmas alone, as she didn't want him to feel obliged to come back and spend it with her.

"But I knew you'd be coming anyway," she chuckled. Again, she had been on the receiving end of another message from Eugene.

By the time Richard returned to Australia, he felt as though he had complied with his uncle's wishes and had afforded him some much-needed peace. He had helped his family through a difficult time—both his living family and his passed Uncle Eugene. It gave him a wonderful sense of comfort.

These days, Eugene no longer visits, quite possibly because he has happily moved on. Despite his alarming, skeletal appearance in Richard's dream visitation, Richard knows that he was by no means trying to frighten him. In fact, he remembers the experience almost fondly, as it gave rise to a challenging but wonderful time in his life.

In remembrance of his uncle, Richard and his wife, Amanda honoured him when naming their firstborn son. Little Eamonn proudly sports the middle name of Eugene–a constant reminder not only of a much-loved uncle, but also of a man who refused to rest until he was sure that his family was okay.

Richard and Amanda with children, Eamonn and Niamh

Chapter Eighteen

A Sibling in Spirit

Prior to commencing a séance, I always warn my sitters that they may not make contact with the spirit they are expecting. And although it hasn't happened to date, I also mention the possibility that no spirits may come through at all. Thus warned, I hope that my sitters come to the table with an open attitude, as it is this relaxed mindset that often gives rise to the most rewarding spirit communications.

Emma arrived at my office brimming with excitement. Our meeting had been postponed twice in the preceding weeks, and we were both glad to finally meet up. Although I gave her my usual pre-séance warning, we were both confident that the morning would be eventful. Especially since Emma is mediumistic herself and seems to attract her fair share of ghostly hangers on! The reason for her paranormal abilities became apparent as the session unfolded.

As we sat at the table and began focussing our energy, the presence of spirits felt immediately palpable. The first spirit to step forward did so without hesitation. He introduced himself as Charlie. He told us that he was Emma's grandfather and that he was taking care of Emma together with Elsie.

"And who's Elsie?" I asked.

NAN, answered Charlie.

Somewhat taken aback, Emma confirmed that Charlie and Elsie were her grandparents. The threesome proceeded to have a heart-warming conversation, with Charlie and Elsie readily responding to the questions that Emma put forward. They answered every question correctly, dispelling any doubt with regards to the authenticity of the communication. Emma was convinced that her grandparents were with us at the table.

After a while, their energy began to get sluggish, so I asked if there was anyone else connected to Emma who would like to speak to us. The affirmative response came back strongly. We bid our farewells to Emma's charming grandparents and waited for the next spirit to come through.

Charlie and Elsie

A young man came forward and introduced himself as James, and I could tell by Emma's reaction that he was someone that she recognised. When he told us that he was Emma's brother, I caught my breath. I had no idea that she had lost someone so close. I asked James how old he was when he passed away, so that Emma could confirm that he was indeed her brother. The planchette sped across the table, and sat above the number 0.

I looked up at Emma for confirmation.

"He was stillborn," said Emma.

Emma's mother went into premature labour twenty weeks into her pregnancy, and James had already passed away before he entered this world. Emma herself was also born prematurely and was delivered into the world at only twenty-three weeks gestation. Even with current medical advances, babies born so early struggle to survive. Twenty-eight years ago survival was even more unlikely, which makes it nothing short of miraculous that she survived such a precarious start to life.

When I considered this later, I wondered if it was Emma's near death experience which gave rise to her paranormal abilities. I believe that my own premature delivery brought about my clairvoyance, so it was possible that Emma's start to life may have similarly increased her sensitivity to the other side.

And now, all these years later, Emma was connecting with the brother who passed away the year before she was born. James' energy was strong and vibrant; it seemed he had been eagerly waiting to speak to his younger sister.

"How old are you now, James?" I asked.

29

Emma and I smiled at each other as she confirmed that this was correct. It was heartening to know that James was a crossed-over spirit, which we knew by the fact that he had continued to mature. By contrast, if someone doesn't cross over and stays in the ghost state, they remain as they were at death. A spirit, however, can manifest at any age they like. For babies and children, they usually choose to continue aging until they reach what they perceive to be their prime. An elderly person, on the other hand, will generally present as much younger and more attractive than they were at the time of their death!

We asked James if he was happy, to which he unhesitatingly responded *YES*.

He told us that he was fulfilling his predestined role as a spirit guide; it had been his intended journey all along.

"Are you my guide?" asked Emma.

NO.

"Whose then?"

As the name *TARREN* was spelt out, Emma gasped. She told me that Tarren is the name of her three-year-old son. Knowing that her brother was her son's spirit guide filled her with joy.

James went on to provide a wealth of information, which convinced us both that he was involved in the day-to-day lives of Emma's family. He knew the names of family members and pertinent dates and the fact that Emma and her husband were in the process of moving house.

James' humour was also quick to come through, and he assured us that he had grown into a handsome young man!

By the time the session concluded, it felt as though a lot of healing had taken place. What had been a tragic chapter in Emma's family history had evolved into something beautiful. As James, Charlie and Elsie said their goodbyes, it felt as though they were heading home after a delightful family reunion. The energy they left in their wake was nothing short of joyous.

Emma was delighted to discover that her deceased brother was now her son's spirit guide.

So even though I try to discourage my sitters from expecting too much from a spirit contact session, I have yet to come across someone who is disappointed by the spirits who do turn up. Those who need to hear certain messages from spirit will receive them, and those who need nothing more than proof of the afterlife unreservedly receive this gift. And some, like Emma, will receive the precious gift of healing and the knowledge that the loving bonds of family never die. The tragedies of life are not always as they seem, they are the stories of souls playing out exactly as they should. Stories which always have a happy ending.

Chapter Nineteen

The Eye-Candy Ghost

My friend, Lidia, whom many consider to be a ghost magnet, seems to have attracted otherworldly visitors for as long as she can remember. Her earliest memories are similar to my own, whereby her ghostly encounters were just a normal part of life. As she got older, however, her visitations suddenly began to feel frightening. Lidia's natural acceptance of the spirit world began to give way to fear, as societal attitudes towards the paranormal tainted her own feelings towards ghosts. All of a sudden Lidia began perceiving the ghosts as frightening, whereas in reality, the ghosts were exactly as they always had been. It was Lidia who had changed.

As is often the case with the spiritually sensitive, Lidia has now gone the full circle and has embraced the spirit world once again. As with me, there was a turning point, whereby the realisation dawned on her that ghosts are nowhere near as frightening as we imagine them to be. In fact, embracing the ability to interact with ghosts is a life-enhancing gift that brings a great deal of comfort and healing. It reminds us that life goes on after death.

For me, the pivotal event which saw me begin to accept the spirit world was when my dear friend, Deni, passed away. Deni and I had been close since our first year at university, and I was devastated by his death at thirty years of age.

Deni's untimely passing had me wishing that he would visit me; my desire to see him again was stronger than my once-consuming fear.

When he first started connecting with me, Deni's visits were vivid enough to stop me in my tracks. They were not, however, confronting in the slightest. If anything, Deni's visits were imbued with humour and good will and invariably made me feel as though I was still strongly connected to my dear friend. These days, I don't think of him as dead at all; it feels more as though he is just living somewhere far away.

I have no doubt that Deni is entirely responsible for my change in attitude towards spirits, and for this, I am truly indebted to him.

Lidia was similarly eased back towards an acceptance of the spirit world by a benevolent spirit, whom coincidentally, also happened to be the ghost of a handsome young man.

Lidia was fifteen years old and living in the far north of Western Australia with her parents and three siblings. Since their small rental only had two bedrooms, Lidia and her two sisters had to share a bedroom. Given that they were soon to discover that their house was haunted, this wasn't such a bad thing!

The town of Karratha is renowned for its hot year-round weather, with an average daily temperature of around 40 degrees Celsius. Before the days of widespread air conditioning (which is when Lidia and her family lived there), the only chance of being comfortable enough to sleep was to open the blinds and the windows and hope for a breeze. Despite doing so each evening before they went to bed, the girls would repeatedly wake up in a hot and stuffy bedroom. Without fail, their blinds would be drawn into darkness and the windows were tightly shut. Of course the sisters blamed each other.

"My sister was convinced it was me," laughed Lidia. "No matter how much I denied it, she'd go off and whinge to Mum."

The mystery was solved one night, when Lidia was awoken sometime before daybreak. She was roused by the sound of footsteps, so she opened her eyes and peered into the moonlit room.

"At first he just looked like a dark shadow," said Lidia. "But the more I looked, the clearer he became. He began to look more and more solid."

Lidia described the man as being around twenty years old, with well-built arms and a 'six-pack'. She said that he was shirtless, barefooted and wearing a pair of jeans. From what she could make out in the moonlight, he was very good looking.

As Lidia watched from beneath the sheet, the man crossed the room towards one of her sisters. He stopped abruptly as he reached the end of her bed and leaned down towards her. It was as if he was checking up on her. He then did the same to the other sister.

By now, Lidia was barely able to breathe, as she fully expected that the man would walk over and do the same to her. Instead, he headed towards the window, swiftly closing it and then pulling down the blinds.

As Lidia watched in awe, he walked towards a small gap beside the cupboard, and a moment later he was gone.

"He just disappeared into this small, dark crack," said Lidia. "And that's the moment I knew beyond a doubt, that I'd just been watching a ghost."

Lidia says that the ghost continued to shut the blinds and windows night after night, and she believes that he was just trying to keep the family safe. At no time did he feel ominous or threatening. He did, however, increase his ghostly repertoire, and would frequently mess with the lights, turning them on and off whenever he saw fit.

Of particular amusement were the television set and video recorder, both of which he tampered with, with ruthless abandon. Video cassettes would fast forward in the middle of a movie, no doubt causing him no end of amusement as the outraged teenagers roared with complaint. The television habitually turned itself on in the middle of the night, loud enough to wake the deepest sleeper.

Since the family had rented both the TV and video machine shortly before the electrical manifestations started, their first thought was that the two items must've been faulty. They called the rental company who were happy to replace them, yet still, the disturbances continued.

"The weird thing is, we weren't even scared. The ghost gave off the feeling that he was just as much a part of the household as we were."

Interestingly, the paranormal activity was not confined to Lidia's family home, and there was considerable talk of ghosts throughout the immediate neighbourhood.

"The belief was that something untoward had happened close by," said Lidia. "Some kind of tragedy. I'm not sure if it was same guy going from house to house, or if there were a few of them. But we thought that there must have been some kind of accident or something."

"A road accident?" I asked.

"I'm not sure," said Lidia. "We never managed to find out."

It certainly didn't seem as though Lidia's ghost was trapped or distraught, if anything he seemed to enjoy lingering amongst the living. It was as if he had taken on the roles of both protector and joker. From Lidia's perspective, it certainly didn't hurt that he was easy on the eye! It made the whole concept of a ghost seem less ominous.

The episode taught Lidia that the living and the dead can indeed live side-by-side and that ghostly manifestations needn't be confronting. Much of our reactions are based on our expectations and attitudes, and adjusting these within ourselves makes negative experiences less likely.

So although the good-looking young ghost frequently had Lidia and her sisters cooking in their beds, she recalls his regular visits fondly.

"Except for the video player," she laughs. "Now that really ticked me off!"

Lidia has been experiencing the paranormal for as long as she can remember. Although initially unsettled by the presence of spirits, the attentions of a handsome young spirit soon changed her mind.

Chapter Twenty

Transition

If anecdotal accounts of deathbed visitations are anything to go by, the process of dying is not the lonely experience we sometimes imagine it to be. I have had the privilege of hearing numerous first hand accounts of those who have been with their loved ones when they have passed, and they invariably share a common theme. It seems more than coincidental that the dying often seem to develop an awareness of long-dead family members in the days or hours before they pass. They may consistently gaze in a particular corner of the room, or engage in lengthy conversations with what appears to be thin air. They are often overcome by a sudden sense of serenity, which seems directly-related to their otherworldly visitors.

Stories such as these (in addition to accounts relayed by those who have survived near-death experiences) suggest that dying souls are lovingly guided to the next level of existence. It has long been believed that this is the case, and indeed accounts of such death-bed interactions further support the likelihood that it's true. But further to this, I believe that the family spirits who come to escort the dying towards the light also have a significant role in supporting the living. A recent conversation with my dear friend, Anita, has cemented my belief that this is indeed true.

Although Anita has always had an awareness of the spirit realm, her abilities go through phases of varying sensitivity. At times she is acutely aware of the presences around her, whilst at other times she just has a vague sense of the spirit world. There is no rhyme nor reason for her varying abilities, and I experience similar ebbs and flows myself. Perhaps it is par for the course for any mediumistic person, but at times it gives rise to considerable frustration. This is never more true than when one is hoping to feel the presence of one spirit in particular.

Anita's mother was extremely ill, and the family were warned that it wouldn't be long before she passed away. Being one of six daughters, Anita found great comfort and support from her sisters. This was in spite of the fact that together with their mother, they lived on the other side of the world.

Anita and her dear mother

Through the course of her mother's illness, Anita flew home to the UK as often as she could. She was adamant that she would spend quality time with her family in her mother's final months. Never one to beat around the bush, Anita asked her mother whether she would visit her when she passed. She assured her heartbroken daughter that she would.

Anita's sisters are also blessed with a similar sensitivity, and indeed seemed to be experiencing an upsurge in visitations since their mother became ill. Anita couldn't help feeling a little disconcerted when they spoke of being visited by their dear father, who had passed away some eighteen months before. She wondered if her father would also visit her and worried as to whether or not she would be sensitive enough to pick up on his presence.

One sister described her father as a vivid apparition, appearing as he had been in his middle-aged prime. Despite being very frail and afflicted by dementia when he died, he appeared as his sturdy, eloquent self of days gone by. He told his daughter that he loved her, and of course, she was thrilled.

Despite knowing that she probably shouldn't do so, Anita's sister couldn't resist asking about the welfare of her mother. She was desperate for an assurance that she would survive her illness. But as soon as she asked the question, her father began to step back. He held up his hand in an attempt to halt the question and smiled sadly as he shook his head. Although he didn't say a word, the sister knew he had come to fetch their mother.

Despite the fact that her parents had been divorced for over thirty years, they had remained good friends. Their shared love for their children had bonded them for most of their adult lives. Although not the most likely candidate to come and collect their mother, on some level it made perfect sense. Her father was fulfilling the dual role of helping their mother transition, as well as supporting his soon-to-be orphaned children. Suddenly it all started to feel okay. Anita's sister knew that her mother would soon be relieved of her pain and suffering; perhaps wanting to hold her back on the earth plane was selfish.

Other sisters also reported visits from their father, and Anita couldn't understand why her sensitivity had suddenly dulled. Why did it desert her when she needed it most?

Then one night, it was Anita's turn.

She had not long been off the phone to her mother and was feeling upset that she had sounded so unwell. The family could no longer deny that their mother's time on earth was drawing to an end. Despite their spiritual awareness, it was a harsh and painful blow.

Anita was in the kitchen drying dishes when she was suddenly overcome by a strong and unmistakable presence.

"The whole room just felt as though it was filled with vibration," she said. "It felt as though the air had somehow suddenly become thick." Having felt this shift in the atmosphere of a room many times before, I knew exactly what Anita meant. We both felt similarly excited as she continued with her story.

Anticipating more, Anita's senses were acutely primed; she had no idea what to expect. Then, in one swift motion, she was enveloped in a strong, all-encompassing embrace.

"It was icy," she said. "But it felt really comforting." Anita smiled at the recollection. "Someone was trying to tell me that everything was okay."

"I'm not sure if it was my dad, but whoever it was, was definitely trying to comfort me."

I told her that I was pretty sure that her visitor had indeed been her father, and she smiled from ear to ear. She was not only delighted to be comforted by her adored father, but she felt that the visit signified a resurgence of her spiritual sensitivity. So perhaps when her mother did cross over into the spirit world, Anita would be in tune with her energy too. Knowing that her father was waiting for her mother went some way toward making her impending loss feel just that little bit less painful. We both smiled as we imagined their reunion on the other side.

Would her mother be surprised to be greeted by her ex-husband? Or would their past differences be put behind them in preference for the love which initially bound them? Having retained an amicable relationship, we concluded that Anita's mother would be pleasantly surprised.

"I'm sure that her darling brother is waiting for her too," smiled Anita. "And her bestie!"

It seems that when the time comes, Anita's mother will have quite an entourage waiting to greet her!

So as Anita and her sisters brace for their mother's imminent departure, it is comforting to know that their father is supporting them all in this life-changing transition.

Stories such as Anita's remind us that we are all much more loved and protected than we can ever truly fathom.

This is never more true than when we are faced with pain and adversity, as that's when the spirit world draws in most closely. Our loved ones never leave us, and perhaps they become even closer to us after they die. When my time comes, I look forward to performing a similar role for my family.

The world is not the harsh and unforgiving place it sometimes seems to be. The spirit world makes sure of that.

Chapter Twenty-One

New Beginnings

Many people report the onset of extrasensory abilities following the death of a loved one. It seems that some spirits will go to great lengths to make their presence known to those they have left behind, and this in turn opens up the bereaved to all manner of paranormal experiences.

People who have never experienced the paranormal may suddenly attract a barrage of ghostly visits, both from their departed loved one and anyone else who may be passing by. This was certainly the case with my elderly patient, Dorothy, whose first spirit encounter I wrote about in my first book. Dorothy's first visitation was from her beloved husband, Joe, and she has been routinely experiencing the paranormal ever since. Two years after her first visit from Joe, I called her to see how she was getting on. I wanted to ask whether she was still receiving the odd visit.

"Oh yes!" she laughed. "It's been happening to me ever since. And it's not just Joe who comes by either."

Dorothy told me about her most recent visitor, whom she described as a massive, dark man. To my mind, Dorothy's visitor sounded menacing, but she insisted that she didn't feel scared.

"Ghosts have never worried me," she said matter-of-factly.

Dorothy said that the man came into her bedroom wearing a hat and a long, dark raincoat. It looked as though he had just come in from the rain.

"He also had a walking stick," she said. "So not only could I see him as plain as day, but I could hear his stick banging on the floorboards as he walked towards me."

I asked whether he looked filmy or solid, to which Dorothy replied that he looked very real indeed.

"At first I just assumed he was a real man," she said. "But it didn't take long before it sunk in that he was a ghost and I just thought – Oh well, here we go again!"

The man walked towards Dorothy's bedside. Strangely, she didn't feel at all perturbed by the fact that he was a ghost, if anything, realising that he wasn't an intruder was a relief. She was more affronted by the fact that he had come into her bedroom without her permission.

"What are you doing in here?" she asked crossly. "I don't know you; you shouldn't be here!"

The man turned to her with a look of ill-disguised disdain. It almost felt as though Dorothy should have known who he was, but to this day, she has no idea.

"And then," she gasped with mock horror, "he had the cheek to read through the notes I keep beside my bed! He placed his thumb on the corner of the notepad, and just stood there reading."

Dorothy told me that she often writes herself little reminder notes, or simply jots down her thoughts throughout the course of the day. Having this stranger read through her personal business left her feeling affronted. She made no bones about telling the nosey ghost exactly how she felt.

"And then he just turned around and started to walk away," said Dorothy. But before he made it even half way across the room, Dorothy's late night visitor seemed to simply melt into the ground.

Although she wasn't scared, Dorothy did admit to feeling strangely affected by the experience, even more so when she turned on the light to see the corner of her notes were wet where the ghost had touched them.

I confessed that I would have been more than a little shaken up by such a visitor, but Dorothy assured me that she felt quite safe.

"Besides," she said, "I'm protected by the angels. Did I tell you about them?"

With little encouragement, Dorothy launched into another recent experience, which happened on the night before she was due to have some skin cancers removed.

"I was really worried," she said, "I had these awful cancers on my chin and they needed to be cut out. Somehow I finally managed to get to sleep, but I woke up not long after with the feeling that someone was in my room."

Dorothy awoke to the vision of her room being filled with smoke and immediately panicked. Her first thought was that her house was on fire.

"I thought that someone might have left the stove on, so I quickly grabbed my dressing gown and started heading to the kitchen."

Before she had gotten even half way across her bedroom, the smoke instantly cleared. She could now see with more lucidity than she could in the daylight and the realisation left her baffled.

"And then I saw this beautiful angel!" she said. "She made me feel absolutely wonderful!"

Dorothy said that although the angel didn't actually speak to her, she felt as though the angel was communicating with her telepathically.

"She wanted me to know that everything was going to be alright."

Dorothy said that the angel extended her hand towards her, and as she did so, Dorothy felt like the most adored person in the world.

"I just knew that she loved me. She was so beautiful."

Dorothy said the next thing she knew was that she was lying safely back in her bed, but she was convinced that it hadn't been a dream. Especially since another angel came and repeated the same sequence of events the very next night. With the surgery out of the way, Dorothy took the second visit as an assurance that the biopsy results would be favourable, as indeed they were.

"The second angel was beautiful too. I really wish they'd visit me again."

The angels' assurances that Dorothy would be fine were of course true, and Dorothy's cancers were removed without incident or repercussions. Of course, deep down Dorothy knew that she'd be fine, but it was lovely to think that even something as minor as an old lady's worries were important enough to warrant the attentions of angels. It's a heart-warming thought!

Chapter Twenty-Two

Spouses in Spirit

A common question with regard to the afterlife is: what happens when widows and widowers remarry? Do their deceased spouses disapprove of their new unions? And who do the widowed ultimately end up with in the spirit world– their first spouse or their most recent one? Or can one remain married to both?

As to what happens on the other side, until such time that we are spirits ourselves, we can do little more than hypothesize. I do believe, however, that relationships in the spirit world aren't bound by earthly constraints, and I am dubious about the concept of marriage continuing in spirit. I believe that we incarnate (and also reincarnate) within our unique soul group, which is the spirit world's equivalent of an earthly family. So whilst one's spouse on the earth plane may no longer be married to that person after death, they are likely to be from the same soul group and will therefore remain eternally connected.

For those couples in destructive or inharmonious unions, it's more likely that they are not from the same soul group. They have, however, entered into a difficult marriage with each other as part of a pre-incarnation agreement. Their marriage is for the purposes of promoting spiritual growth as opposed to being a bond borne of camaraderie and love. Although it is designed to achieve a higher purpose, since the couple are unlikely to be from the same soul group, their deaths herald the end of their unified journey.

But what of those who are indeed well-suited and genuinely in love? What happens to their bond should the surviving spouse choose to remarry? Would the departed husband or wife feel affronted to see their partner moving on with someone else? According to my friend, Karen, it seems that the opposite is more likely to be true.

Karen and her husband, Ray, had been married for four years when he was diagnosed with advanced bowel cancer. He was only thirty years old. Karen and Ray's relationship had been harmonious but fraught with tragedy as both of Karen's pregnancies had ended in miscarriage at around sixteen weeks gestation.

Karen tells me that Ray's health deteriorated quickly after his diagnosis, and he passed away the following year. In the lead up to his death, Ray often made comments which

Karen considered to be obtuse and peculiar. Although looking back now, they make perfect sense.

"I just thought he was getting delirious," said Karen. "He often used to ask me if I could see the white light in the corner of the room... and he'd point out his grandfather and two small children. I suppose they must have been the children that we lost."

Not as spiritually aware as she is now, Karen didn't fully absorb the importance of Ray's pre-death visions. In retrospect, she appreciates their significance, and indeed recalling them now is a source of great comfort.

Ray had also spoken about his four-year-old niece, Tiffany.

"Tell her not to draw on the computer," he said.

Karen was baffled. As far as she was aware, Tiffany hadn't drawn on the computer at all. Since Karen knew full well that her niece would never do such a thing, she didn't bother to raise the matter with her young niece. It wasn't mentioned again until after Ray passed away.

Ray's sister, who was Tiffany's mother, rang Karen in some confusion. It had been close to a year since Ray's death.

"I don't even know if this makes sense, but I need to tell you something," she said. "Tiffany says that Uncle Ray came to visit. It seems he wanted to say sorry."

Karen couldn't imagine why Ray would want to apologise. But as her sister-in-law continued to speak, the pieces fell into place.

"Tiffany says he's sorry for saying that she drew on the computer. He knows now that she didn't do it..."

Even though Karen's sister-in-law didn't know what to make of her daughter's revelation, from Karen's point-of-view, it made complete sense. It was the first time that Ray had made his presence known to his family, and he has continued to do so ever since.

Although Ray's visitations are somewhat sporadic, they happen frequently enough for Karen to feel as though Ray is still around her. As the following episodes attest, it seems that he is more than happy for his wife to be getting on with her life—new husband and all.

In 2009, Karen's second husband, Mark, began experiencing the symptoms of what he believed was a heart attack. With a sickening sense of deja vu, Karen rushed Mark to the local medical clinic. After monitoring and testing, cardiac arrest was quickly ruled out. Rather than feeling relieved, however, Karen felt increasingly uneasy. It was obvious that something was very wrong. A moment later, Karen's fears were confirmed like a bolt from the blue. An unseen someone (whom she soon discovered was Ray) suddenly gave her hair a sharp tug. Then, as clearly as if he were still alive, he whispered in Karen's ear, *Check his PSAs!*

To the ill-disguised surprise of both Mark and his doctor, Karen repeated Ray's whispered request. She had asked for Mark's PSAs to be tested before she'd even processed exactly what she was saying. (PSAs are prostate-specific antigens, and an elevated level of the protein in a blood test may be indicative of prostate cancer.)

Since Mark was having a battery of blood tests anyway, his doctor had no reservations in adding the PSA request to the list. Some days later, the test results came back positive. Mark was diagnosed with early stage prostate cancer. Due to early intervention, the disease was able to be treated without serious repercussions.

A year later, Ray saw fit to intervene again. As part of a government initiative to reduce the mortality rates of bowel cancer, all Australians over the age of fifty were sent a bowel cancer testing kit in the mail. Mark had received one of the screening kits, and it sat unused on the kitchen table for over a month. When Karen questioned him about it, he said that he'd decided not to bother with it as he had no reason to suspect there were any issues with his bowel. No sooner had Mark made his announcement, than the test kit came flying off the table. It landed several feet away on the opposite side of the kitchen, dropping to the floor right in front of Mark's feet.

Needless to say, he took this as a sign, and the test kit was on its way to be analysed a few days later. Perhaps not surprisingly, the test came back positive, and Ray had managed to ensure an early cancer diagnosis for Mark once again. Thankfully the diagnosis had been made early enough to ensure a positive outcome.

Karen has no doubt that her first husband played an indispensable role in protecting the health of his successor. Perhaps Ray wanted to make sure that his wife didn't have to endure the pain of losing a husband yet again.

It seems that our earthly insecurities and petty jealousies are shed when we become spirits and that we are able to view our relationships more selflessly. So even though we may feel unhappy about seeing our partner with someone new whilst we are living, death offers us a more altruistic perspective. Once ego is taken out of the equation, it is our partner's happiness which is paramount. The fact that we have been replaced is viewed as a positive, as our loved one isn't left to negotiate life in solitude and grief.

Ray demonstrated this viewpoint perfectly by saving the life of his widow's new husband not once, but twice. It's an inspiring thought. Despite the fact that I have a reputation of being a jealous Croatian, I know that when I pass to spirit, I will wish the same for my husband. I wish him love and companionship with a new partner... as long as she's up to scratch!

Conclusion

As this collection of true experiences attests, the spectrum of paranormal experiences varies greatly from person to person. Some people are in tune enough to notice subtle signs from departed loved ones, picking up on the gentle assurances that they remain a part of their lives. Perhaps the signs they offer are a little more obvious to ensure that we are aware that they're around. Of course our loved ones are careful not to manifest too ardently, lest they unsettle us!

Less benevolent presences may pull out all the stops, waging heart-stopping displays to convince us of their presence. It is these types of manifestations which give the spirit world a bad reputation, as they are likely to set our hearts (and our limbs) racing. Although usually not malevolent in nature, they are dramatic enough to inspire a reaction—at least this is certainly the case with me!

Despite fervently believing in the spirit world, many people feel that they have yet to receive proof of its existence. They lament their lack of ghostly visitations and wonder what can be done to enhance the probability of a paranormal experience. Reading a book such as this is a valuable first step. Firstly, because it provides examples of the signs you should be looking for. Also, by holding a book such as this in your hands, you announce to the universe that you are interested in other dimensions. Believe me, the spirits get very excited when you read about them!

So read, explore and talk about the other side, and most of all, remember to acknowledge! Validating a visitation with a *thanks* or a *hi* provides an impetus for the spirits to visit us even more. Acknowledging your spirit visitors is the greatest gift you can give them, even if on occasion you get it wrong and are acknowledging thin air! And remember, the spirit world is more respectful than many people realise, so if you're not in the mood for visitors, it's also fine to ask them to go away!

Our world is a truly amazing place—both its seen and unseen facets. Embracing the unseen enhances the experience of life, as it brings with it the knowledge that death is but a transition. A return to realms which are really our home.

32663694R00138

Made in the USA
Middletown, DE
13 June 2016